# OCR GCSE
# Physical Education

**Matthew Hunter**

OXFORD
UNIVERSITY PRESS

# OXFORD

UNIVERSITY PRESS

Great Clarendon Street, Oxford, OX2 6DP, United Kingdom

Oxford University Press is a department of the University of Oxford.

It furthers the University's objective of excellence in research, scholarship, and education by publishing worldwide. Oxford is a registered trade mark of Oxford University Press in the UK and in certain other countries

British Library Cataloguing in Publication Data

Data available

978-0-19-842377-5

3 5 7 9 10 8 6 4

Paper used in the production of this book is a natural, recyclable product made from wood grown in sustainable forests.
The manufacturing process conforms to the environmental regulations of the country of origin.

Printed and bound by CPI Group (UK) Ltd, Croydon, CR0 4YY

OUP would like to thank Kirk Bizley, Maarit Edy, Fiona Garlick, Nathan Marshall and Danny Thompson for their help in preparing this book for publication.

# Contents

# PERFORMANCE IN PHYSICAL EDUCATION

# 1.1 Applied anatomy and physiology

When you have worked through this chapter, you will have developed knowledge and understanding of:

- the structure and function of the skeletal system
- the structure and function of the muscular system
- movement analysis
- the cardiovascular and respiratory systems
- the effects of exercise on the body systems.

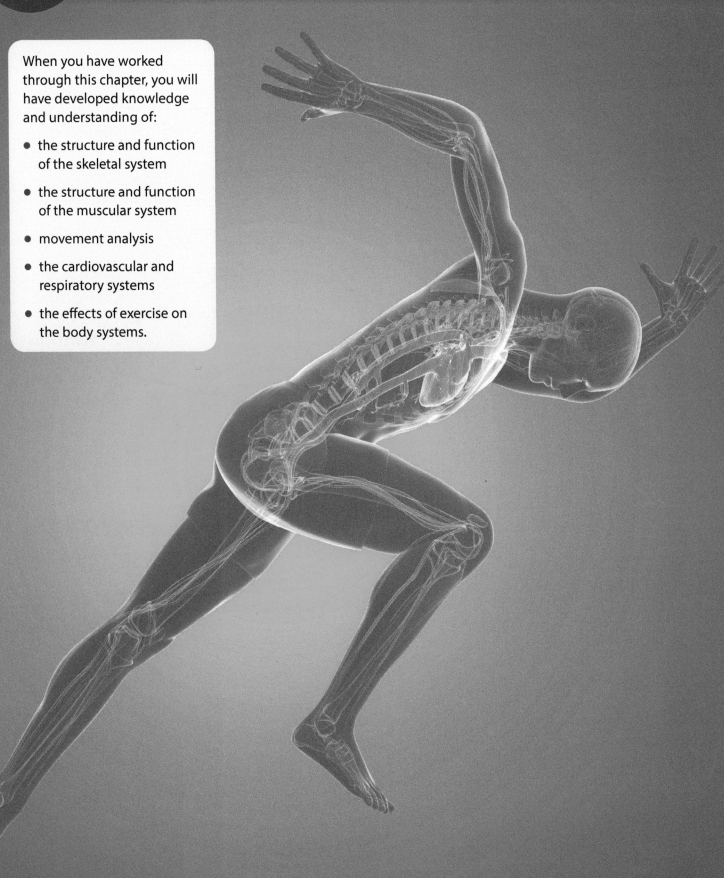

The skeletal system is made up of many bones. While all bones have things in common, the shape of each bone will allow it to fulfil one or more of the **functions of the skeleton**.

### Support

The skeletal system provides a framework to support your muscles and vital organs, keeping them in place so they can function properly. For example, during exercise your skeleton supports your heart, lungs and blood vessels. These work together to provide oxygen to your working muscles, especially during a long-distance activity.

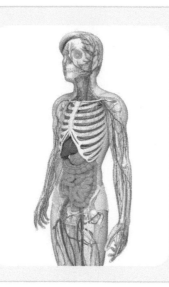

> ### Key term
>
> **Functions of the skeleton:** The skeleton performs six important functions. These are: support, posture, protection, movement, blood cell production and storage of minerals.

**Functions of the skeleton**

### Movement

Without the bones of the skeletal system, you would not be able to move. Bones provide a surface for muscles to attach to via tendons, and provide rigid structures that form levers. When muscles contract, they pull on the bones of the skeleton and movement is achieved. The ability to move is central to all physical activities. For example, the biceps muscle is attached to the radius and ulna by a tendon in the forearm, and when it contracts your elbow flexes.

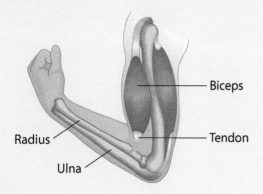

Biceps

Radius

Tendon

Ulna

### Posture

The rigid nature of the bones in the skeletal system allows the body to maintain an upright position and hold the correct shape – the correct posture. For example, you can sit or stand upright because of the vertebral column running through the centre of your body. Many sporting actions require a person to be in an upright position. Good posture also enables you to move your arms and legs freely and, therefore, take part in sporting activities.

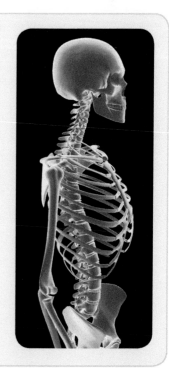

## Protection

Many bones act as a rigid shell. They protect vital organs and the central nervous system, which are soft and easily damaged. During physical activity, protection is crucial for both performance and long-term health. It reduces the chance of injury, which ensures players can continue to train and play. Examples include the cranium protecting the brain when heading a football, and the ribs protecting the heart and lungs during a rugby tackle.

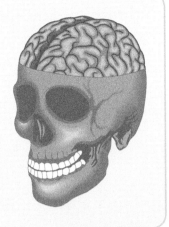

### Study tip

If you can remember 'Bones Make People Perfectly Suit Sports', then you have a memory aid to recall the functions of the skeleton: Blood cell production, Movement, Protection, Posture, Support, Storage of minerals. You could always make up your own memory aid.

## Blood cell production

Red blood cells, white blood cells, and platelets are produced in bone marrow contained within certain bones. Red blood cells are especially important in aerobic activities because they carry oxygen to working muscles. White blood cells fight off infections, and platelets help blood to clot following an injury.

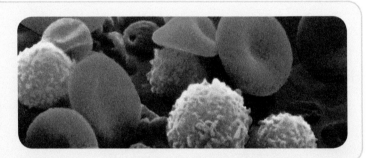

## Storage of minerals

Calcium and phosphorus, along with other minerals, are stored within the bones. These minerals are necessary for vital body functions. For example, calcium and phosphorus are both needed for strong teeth and bones, while calcium is also involved in muscular contractions.

### Activity

1   Look at this photograph and discuss how the different functions of the skeleton are important in rugby.

2   In a group, write down ten sports or physical activities on separate scraps of paper and put them in a hat. Take it in turns to pick an activity out of the hat. Give specific examples of how each function of the skeleton is important in the activity you selected.

The skeletal system is made up of many bones of different shapes and sizes. Different bones can perform different functions in different circumstances. The majority of bones are **articulating bones**, which meet at a joint to allow movement.

## Key term

**Articulating bones:** Bones that move relative to each other at a joint.

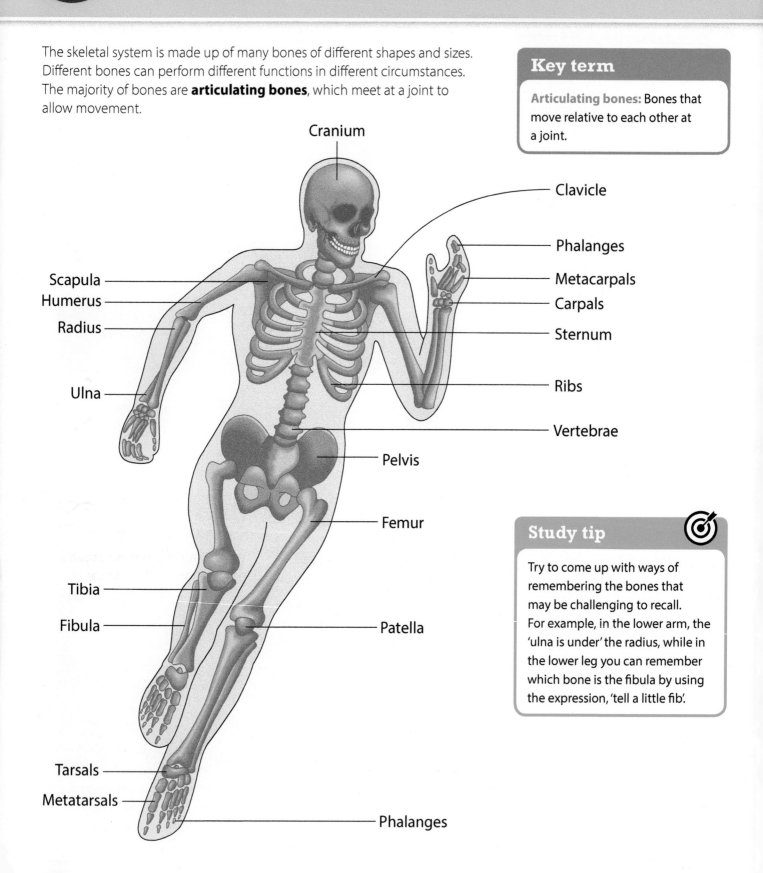

Cranium
Clavicle
Phalanges
Metacarpals
Carpals
Sternum
Scapula
Humerus
Radius
Ribs
Ulna
Vertebrae
Pelvis
Femur
Tibia
Fibula
Patella
Tarsals
Metatarsals
Phalanges

## Study tip

Try to come up with ways of remembering the bones that may be challenging to recall. For example, in the lower arm, the 'ulna is under' the radius, while in the lower leg you can remember which bone is the fibula by using the expression, 'tell a little fib'.

Bones are rigid, so it is the presence of joints that allows movement to occur. Most joints in the human body are freely movable or 'synovial' joints. **Synovial joints** share many common features, but they can be classified according to their structure and the range of movement they allow.

## Hinge joints

The elbow and the knee are hinge joints. Their movement is limited to flexion and extension. They can only move towards and away from each other, increasing or decreasing the angle between the articulating bones, just like a door. They cannot move sideways or in circles.

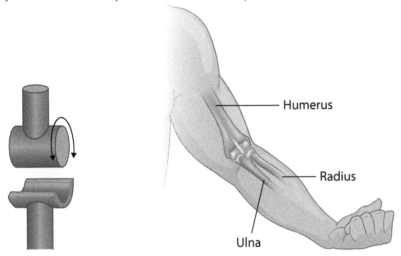
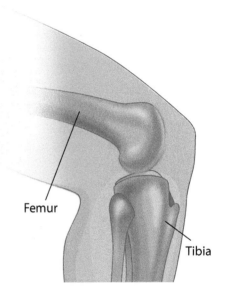

▲ The articulating bones of the elbow joint and the knee joint.

## Ball and socket joints

The shoulder and the hip are ball and socket joints. Their design means they can move in many different directions and provide a large range of movement.

▼ The articulating bones of the shoulder joint and the hip joint.

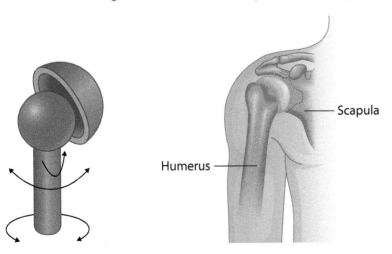
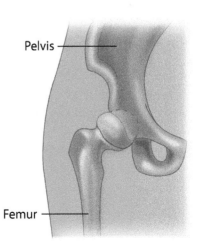

# 1.1.4 Types of movement at joints

While most sporting actions require a combination of movements at a number of joints simultaneously, it is possible to isolate specific joint actions. The different movements at joints are named so that sporting actions can be described and analysed.

When looking at joints, those that can perform many different movement types are seen as having a large range of movement, while those restricted to a low number of movements are considered to have a low range of movement. For example, the knee (a hinge joint) has a limited range of movement, whereas the hip (a ball and socket joint) has a far greater range of movement because it is capable of performing many different movements.

## Movements at hinge joints

Hinge joints can only perform flexion and extension. Movement at hinge joints is limited to increasing and decreasing the angle at the joint.

### Flexion
*working phase*

The angle at a joint is decreased. Flexion can be seen as bending at the hinge joints of the elbow and knee. It happens at the elbow joint when preparing for a chest pass in netball.

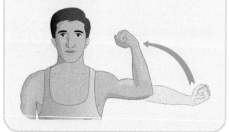

### Extension
*→ relaxingphase*

The angle at a joint is increased. Extension can be seen as straightening at the hinge joints of the elbow and knee. It happens at the elbow joint when executing a smash shot in badminton.

## Activity

3   When shooting a football at goal, a player will demonstrate flexion and extension. Describe the action of shooting a football at goal, identifying when you see flexion and when you see extension. Be sure to name the type of joints and the articulating bones involved in the movement.

4   List as many sporting actions as you can where flexion and/or extension are seen at hinge joints. Include examples that involve both the elbow and knee joints.

# Movements at ball and socket joints

Ball and socket joints have a very open structure, which means that many different sporting movements are possible at the shoulder and the hip, where we have ball and socket joints.

⊗ Star jump

penalty kick

### Flexion

The angle at a joint is decreased. At ball and socket joints, flexion is movement going in a forward direction. This can be seen at the shoulder and the hip. It happens at the hip joint when a sprinter drives their leg forward.

### Extension

The angle of the joint is increased. At ball and socket joints, extension is movement going in a backward direction. This can be seen at the shoulder and the hip. It happens at the hip joint when a rugby player takes their leg back to prepare for a conversion.

### Adduction

Adduction can be seen when a limb is moved back towards the midline of the body at a ball and socket joint. It can be seen at the shoulder and the hip. It happens at the shoulder joint when a swimmer completes the breaststroke arm pull.

### Abduction

Abduction can be seen when a limb is moved away from the midline of the body at a ball and socket joint. It can be seen at the shoulder and the hip. It happens at the hip joint when a trampolinist performs a straddle shape.

### Circumduction

This is a combination of flexion, abduction, adduction and extension and looks like you are drawing a circle in the air. This is possible at the ball and socket joints of the shoulder and the hip. It happens at the shoulder joint when a cricketer bowls a delivery.

### Rotation

This is a twisting action. At the ball and socket joints of the shoulder and hip, rotation takes place when the arm or leg twists along its long axis. It happens at the shoulder joint when playing a drive shot in table tennis, as the arm moves from low to high to apply top spin.

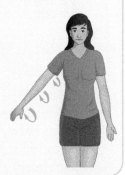

## Activity

5    Prepare a list of movement instructions that your partner can follow in order to perform a skill of your choice. You should start with your partner in the anatomical position. For example, you might start by telling your partner to 'Flex your right elbow.'

## Key terms

**Abduction:** Movement away from the midline of the body.

**Adduction:** Movement towards the midline of the body.

**Circumduction:** A circular movement at a joint that combines flexion, extension, abduction and adduction.

**Rotation:** A twisting action that takes place when a body part turns along its long axis, as if on a pivot.

During sporting actions, three components of synovial joints are crucial if movements are to take place effectively. These are ligaments, cartilage and tendons.

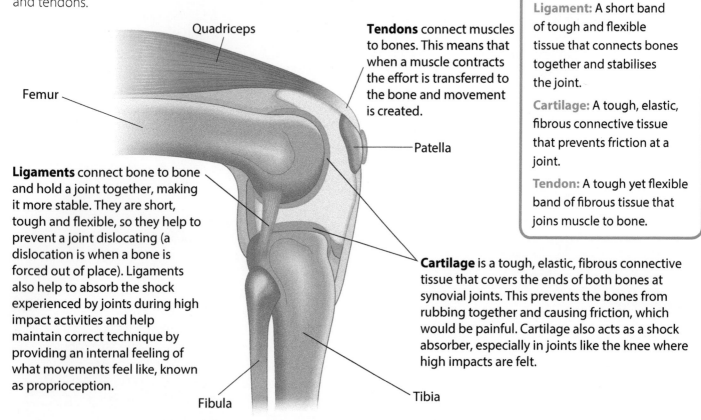

Quadriceps

Femur

Patella

**Tendons** connect muscles to bones. This means that when a muscle contracts the effort is transferred to the bone and movement is created.

**Ligaments** connect bone to bone and hold a joint together, making it more stable. They are short, tough and flexible, so they help to prevent a joint dislocating (a dislocation is when a bone is forced out of place). Ligaments also help to absorb the shock experienced by joints during high impact activities and help maintain correct technique by providing an internal feeling of what movements feel like, known as proprioception.

**Cartilage** is a tough, elastic, fibrous connective tissue that covers the ends of both bones at synovial joints. This prevents the bones from rubbing together and causing friction, which would be painful. Cartilage also acts as a shock absorber, especially in joints like the knee where high impacts are felt.

Fibula

Tibia

## Key terms

**Ligament:** A short band of tough and flexible tissue that connects bones together and stabilises the joint.

**Cartilage:** A tough, elastic, fibrous connective tissue that prevents friction at a joint.

**Tendon:** A tough yet flexible band of fibrous tissue that joins muscle to bone.

## Activity

6   Use a soft modelling material, such as Plasticine or Play-Doh, to make a model of a knee joint, using the diagram above to help you. Use different colours for the ligaments, the tendons and the cartilage. Once complete, talk your partner through what you have made.

7   This squash player is using many joints. Explain, in your own words, the role of his ligaments, tendons and cartilage as he moves to play his shot. What would or would not happen if these components didn't do their jobs properly?

# The location of the major muscle groups

Movement, sporting or otherwise, is produced when skeletal muscles, attached to bones by tendons, contract. Sporting actions are strong examples of the work that the skeletal and muscular systems do. A contracting muscle pulls on a bone, which alters the angle at a joint, and movement is produced.

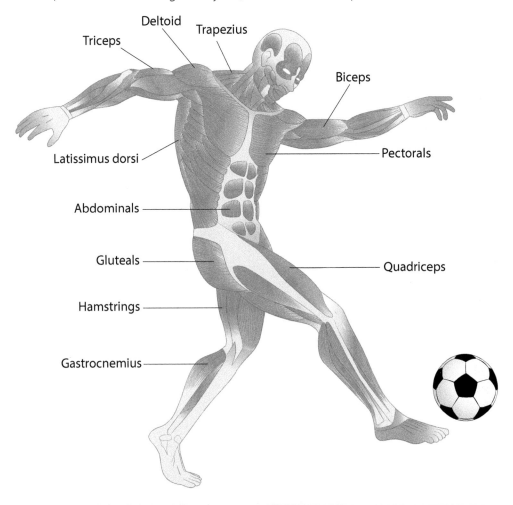

## Activity

8   Investigate the movements that are created at the knee joint, the elbow joint, the shoulder joint and the hip joint when the muscles in the diagram above contract. You'll need to get up and move about in order to work them out. Copy and complete the table to record your findings.

| When this muscle contracts... | ...it causes this movement... | ...of this body part | Sporting example |
|---|---|---|---|
| *When the gluteals contract* | *it causes extension* | *at the hip.* | *Lifting the leg backwards when preparing to kick a football* |

Because muscles can only pull on bones and are not capable of pushing them, they are arranged in pairs on each side of joints. Movement is produced when one muscle contracts and pulls on a bone, while the opposite muscle relaxes and allows the bone to be pulled. The same process happens in the other direction when the other muscle contracts. In this way, a muscle takes on a different role depending on whether it is contracting or relaxing.

## Antagonistic pairs

A pair of muscles is called an antagonistic pair, and they are said to operate with an **antagonistic muscle action**. The muscle contracting is known as the **agonist**, while the opposite muscle, which is relaxing, is known as the **antagonist**.

Other nearby muscles can act as **fixators**, contracting to stabilise other body parts, preventing unintended movements and allowing the agonist to create the intended movement effectively. For example, during both the upward and downward phases of a biceps curl, the deltoid acts as a fixator.

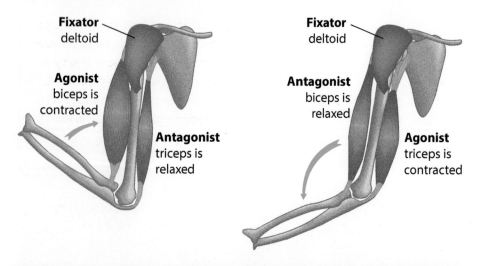

**Fixator**
deltoid

**Agonist**
biceps is
contracted

**Antagonist**
triceps is
relaxed

**Fixator**
deltoid

**Antagonist**
biceps is
relaxed

**Agonist**
triceps is
contracted

◀ The biceps and triceps contract and relax to allow the arm to flex and extend at the elbow.

## Key terms

**Antagonistic muscle action:** A pair of muscles work together to produce movement, with one muscle contracting while the other muscle relaxes. For example, an antagonistic muscle action takes place in the upper arm as the biceps contracts and the triceps relaxes.

**Agonist:** The muscle that works to create a movement.

**Antagonist:** The muscle that works in the opposite way to the agonist, relaxing to allow movement.

**Fixator:** A muscle that acts as a stabilizer, helping the agonist to work effectively to create movement.

◄ Look at this player. He is about to perform a volleyball set. Currently, his elbow joints are slightly flexed. As he executes the set, he needs to extend at the elbows quickly. To do this, the triceps will act as the agonist and contract to pull on the radius and ulna in the forearm. At the same time, the biceps will act as the antagonist and relax. This will allow the bones to be pulled. The biceps and triceps are working as an antagonistic pair. Extension at the elbow will take place, and the player's arms will straighten to produce the set shot.

## Activity

**9 a)** Model the action of the volleyball set and think about your triceps acting as the agonist as your arms extend at the elbow.

**b)** Place one hand around the inside of your opposite upper arm. Now imagine you have something heavy in your free hand, while you perform a biceps curl. As you go through the upward phase, you should feel your biceps getting bigger as it contracts as the agonist, causing flexion at the elbow. You should also feel the triceps getting longer and thinner as it relaxes as the antagonist. Describe what happens when you go through the downward phase of the movement.

**c)** Carry out a similar practical experiment and describe what happens when you flex and extend your left knee while standing on your right leg.

The following muscles make up the most obvious antagonistic pairs:

- biceps and triceps, acting at the elbow to create flexion and extension

- hamstrings and quadriceps, acting at the knee to create flexion and extension.

During sporting situations, antagonistic pairs swap roles continuously. A muscle acts as both an agonist and an antagonist depending on the movement required.

▶ Look at this skier. As he flexes and extends at the knees – to crouch into turns and then stand up again – his hamstrings and quadriceps switch between acting in the role of the agonist and acting in the role of the antagonist.

# 1.1.8 Lever systems

**Levers** are seen in everyday life as well as in sport and exercise. A lever system is a rigid bar that moves around a fixed fulcrum with two forces applied to it. Levers can change the size or direction of the effort used, to make a task more manageable.

All levers consist of three key elements:

1  **Fulcrum:** a fixed pivot point.

2  **Effort:** the source of the energy that will do the work.

3  **Load:** the weight/resistance to be moved.

## Key terms

**Lever:** A rigid bar or object that moves around a fixed fulcrum with two forces applied to it.

**Fulcrum:** A fixed pivot point. For example, a joint in the body.

**Effort:** The source of the energy. For example, muscles in the body.

**Load:** The weight/resistance to be moved. For example, a body part plus anything held or resistance met.

## Activity

10  The picture shows how a lever can be useful.

   **a)** Explain how this lever works and what advantage a person gains from using a lever in this situation.

   **b)** Can you identify the fulcrum, effort and load in the picture?

## First, second and third class levers

There are three **classes of lever**: first class levers, second class levers and third class levers. The class of lever is determined by the position of the fulcrum, load and effort in relation to each other. In the human body, the muscular and skeletal systems create levers around every joint. These allow us to move. The joint acts as the fulcrum, effort comes from contracting muscles and the load is the body part being moved, plus any additional objects held or resistance met. The body contains all classes of lever, but third class levers are most common.

## Key term

**Class of lever:** The type of lever. There are first class, second class and third class levers.

## Study tip

You will need a method for remembering the difference between first, second and third class levers. Try imagining: one see-saw, two wheelbarrows and three fishing rods.

Or use the mnemonic '1, 2, 3, F, L, E' to help you remember the middle element of each class of lever.

| Class of lever | First class lever | Second class lever | Third class lever |
| --- | --- | --- | --- |
| Lever drawing | | | |
| Well-known example for you to remember easily | | | |
| Example in the human body | | | |
| Sporting example | | | |

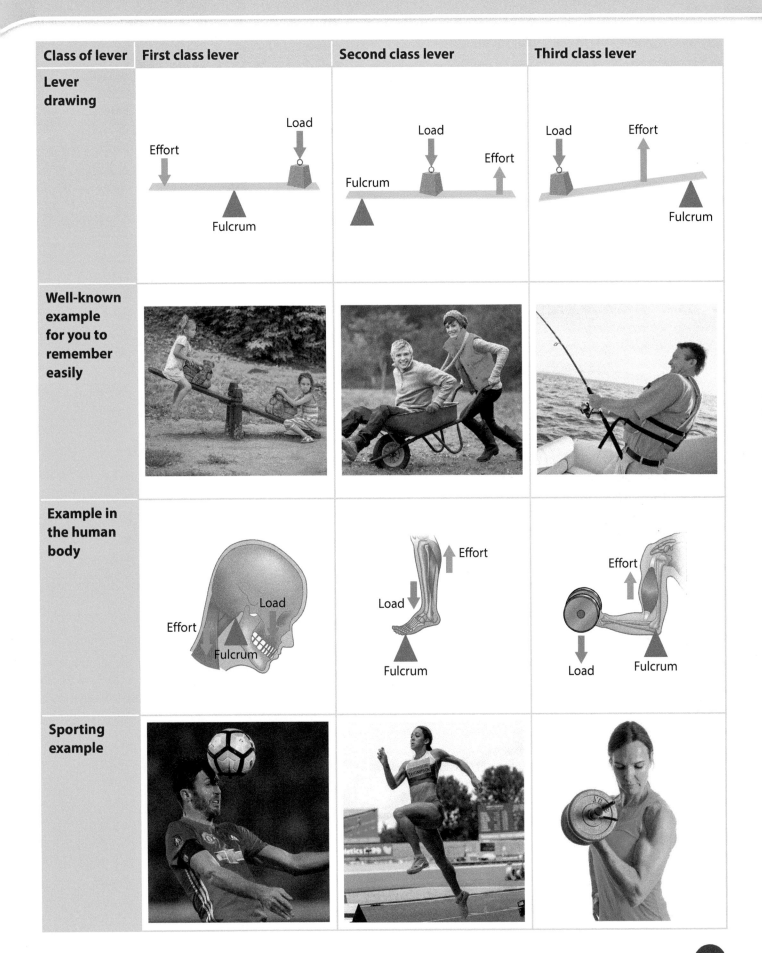

17

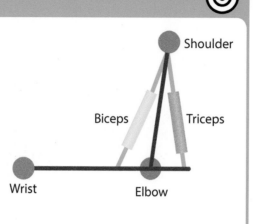

## Levers and mechanical advantage

Some levers have **mechanical advantage**. This means that they are able to move large loads with a relatively small amount of effort.

Levers have two arms: an **effort arm** and a **load arm**. The distance from the fulcrum to the effort is the effort arm, while the distance from the fulcrum to the load is the load arm. Whether a lever has mechanical advantage or not is determined by the relative length of the two arms. If the lever's effort arm is longer than its load arm, it has mechanical advantage.

Because all second class levers have the load in the middle, they all have longer effort arms than load arms. As a result, they all have mechanical advantage. All second class levers are able to move large loads with a relatively small amount of effort.

It is possible for first class levers to have mechanical advantage if the fulcrum is nearer the load than the effort. It is not possible for third class levers to have mechanical advantage.

If we consider a long jumper taking off, we see how the second class lever, where the foot contacts the ground, has mechanical advantage because the effort arm is longer than the load arm. The result of this, for the long jumper, is that the force produced by the muscles, which is relatively small, is able to drive the full weight of the athlete off the ground.

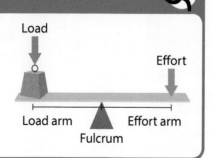

▲ Coaches encourage long jumpers and triple jumpers to have their foot underneath them, rather than in front of them, at take-off. It allows them to maximise the benefits of the second class lever.

Planes of movement and axes of rotation can be used when describing movements. A **plane** is an imaginary line or surface that divides the body into two. Movement occurs in a plane. An **axis** is an imaginary line around which the body rotates.

Planes and axes are both drawn through a body standing in the anatomical position (upright, with arms by the side of the body and palms facing forwards). All movements are then described from this starting point.

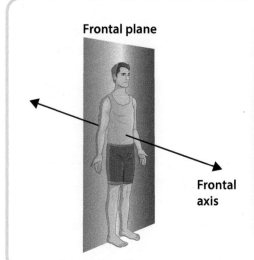

**Frontal plane**

**Frontal axis**

◄ The **frontal plane** divides the body into front and back sections. Movement occurs in the frontal plane around the frontal axis. The **frontal axis** passes through the body from front to back. A cartwheel is a good example of a movement occurring in the frontal plane and around the frontal axis.

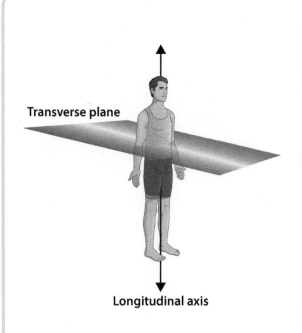

**Transverse plane**

**Longitudinal axis**

◄ The **transverse plane** divides the body into upper and lower sections. Movement occurs in the transverse plane around the longitudinal axis. The **longitudinal axis** passes vertically through the body, allowing rotation of the body in an upright position. A full twist by a trampolinist and a pirouette by an ice-skater are excellent examples of movements occurring in the transverse plane and around the longitudinal axis.

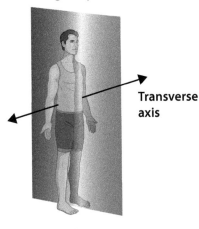

Sagittal plane

Transverse axis

▲ The **sagittal plane** divides the body into left and right sections. Movement occurs in the sagittal plane around the transverse axis. The **transverse axis** passes horizontally through the body from left to right. A front or back somersault in trampolining, diving or gymnastics is a great example of a movement occurring in the sagittal plane and around the transverse axis.

## Key terms

**Frontal plane:** An imaginary line that divides the body from front to back vertically.

**Transverse plane:** An imaginary line that divides the body horizontally into upper and lower sections.

**Sagittal plane:** An imaginary line that divides the body vertically into left and right sides.

**Frontal axis of rotation:** An imaginary line passing horizontally through the body from front to back. A gymnast performing a cartwheel moves around this axis.

**Longitudinal axis of rotation:** An imaginary line passing vertically through the body from top to bottom. A 360 degree turn rotates around this axis.

**Transverse axis of rotation:** An imaginary line passing horizontally through the body from left to right. A somersault moves around this axis.

## Activity

**14 a)** Make a model of a person standing in the anatomical position using a soft modelling material such as Plasticine or Play-Doh. Use a pencil as an axis and two pieces of card as a plane. Push your pencil through your model and attach a piece of card to either side to represent the corresponding plane. If you spin your pencil, the model will rotate around that axis and in line with the plane.

**b)** Can you think of other sporting actions that take place in the planes and around the axes described on these two pages? They can be whole body movements or movements that involve only part of the body.

**c)** Use your model to make a video presentation explaining planes and axes, using the examples you came up with for part b.

## Study tip

A wheel on a bike spins around a central axle. This is how an axis works. If you had an axis through your belly button, you'd spin like a wheel.

Think of a plane as a thick sheet of glass that you're trapped tightly inside. Movements that take place in that plane can only occur in the direction that the sheet of glass allows.

The heart is made up of four chambers. The top two are called **atria** and the bottom two are called **ventricles**. Blood flow through them is guided by one-way valves, of which there are four. The left side of the heart deals with **oxygenated blood** and the right side of the heart accepts and pumps out **deoxygenated blood**.

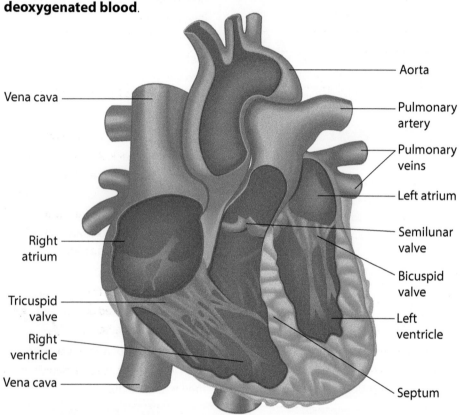

Vena cava

Aorta

Pulmonary artery

Pulmonary veins

Left atrium

Right atrium

Semilunar valve

Tricuspid valve

Bicuspid valve

Right ventricle

Left ventricle

Vena cava

Septum

## Key terms

**Atria:** This is the plural of 'atrium'. There are two atria in the heart. These are the upper chambers of the heart where blood enters.

**Ventricles:** There are two ventricles in the heart. These are the lower chambers of the heart from where blood exits.

**Oxygenated blood:** Blood containing a high concentration of oxygen.

**Deoxygenated blood:** Blood containing a low concentration of oxygen.

## Study tip

The heart is drawn as if you are looking down at it on a table, but it is labelled as if the heart is in your body. The heart's left-hand side is labelled 'left' not the side that you see on the left when you are looking at the diagram. As a result, the labels appear to be the wrong way around; but they're not.

## Activity

15 Make a quick sketch of the heart and label all four chambers, the blood vessels, the valves and the septum. Now draw it several more times, from memory, trying to do it quicker and quicker each time. Each time you finish, look carefully at the labels you forgot to add or got wrong, and try to remember one or two more for your next attempt. After a few attempts, you should find yourself remembering most of the labels correctly.

# 1.1.11 The pathway of blood through the heart

Because the heart beats in a very organised manner, and contains one-way valves that prevent blood flowing in the wrong direction, blood moves through the heart in a very specific way.

> Blood returns from the body through the **vena cava**.

> Deoxygenated blood enters the right atrium.

> Deoxygenated blood passes through the **tricuspid valve** into the right ventricle.

> Deoxygenated blood is pumped through **pulmonary arteries** to the lungs. The **semilunar valves** prevent blood re-entering the heart.

> Blood is oxygenated at the lungs.

> Oxygenated blood returns to the heart through the **pulmonary veins**.

> Oxygenated blood enters the left atrium of the heart.

> Oxygenated blood passes through the **bicuspid valve** and into the left ventricle.

> Oxygenated blood is pumped through the **aorta** to the muscles and organs of the body. The semilunar valves prevent blood re-entering the heart.

## Key terms

**Vena cava:** The large vein entering the right atrium of the heart that carries deoxygenated blood back from the body to the heart.

**Tricuspid valve:** A one-way gate that separates the right atrium from the right ventricle.

**Pulmonary artery:** The artery that carries deoxygenated blood from the heart to the lungs.

**Semilunar valves:** One-way gates at the entrance to the aorta and pulmonary artery, which prevent the backflow of blood into the heart.

**Pulmonary vein:** The vein that carries oxygenated blood from the lungs to the heart.

**Bicuspid valve:** A one-way gate that separates the left atrium from the left ventricle.

**Aorta:** The artery that carries blood from the heart to the rest of the body.

## Activity

16 Find a big space and create a huge diagram of the heart using cones. Make sure your heart has outer walls and all the blood vessels and valves are in place. Walk through the diagram, starting at the point where the vena cava enters the heart, describing your route as you take it. Take this book with you to check that the details are correct.

## Study tip

The volumes of blood that the heart pumps out, and how blood circulation is affected by exercise, are covered on page 27.

The heart pumps blood to two destinations at the same time, using a double-circulatory system. This system ensures that a continuous flow of oxygenated blood reaches the muscles and organs.

- Pulmonary circulation takes deoxygenated blood from the heart to the lungs, where it becomes oxygenated, before returning it to the heart.

- Systemic circulation takes oxygenated blood from the heart to the rest of the body, where it becomes deoxygenated as it delivers the oxygen it carries to the muscles and organs, before returning it to the heart.

### Activity

**17** Discuss this diagram with a partner. Can you describe what it shows?

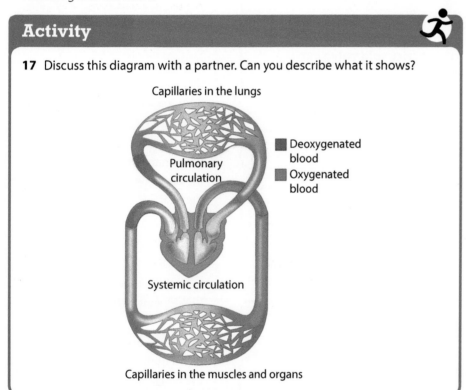

Capillaries in the lungs

Pulmonary circulation

Systemic circulation

Capillaries in the muscles and organs

■ Deoxygenated blood
■ Oxygenated blood

### Key term

**Red blood cells:** Oxygen carrying cells containing haemoglobin.

## The role of red blood cells in oxygen transport

Both circulatory networks rely on blood to carry oxygen. Blood contains **red blood cells**, which are crucial for transporting oxygen around the body.

Red blood cells contain haemoglobin, a protein that allows oxygen to bind to it and be carried. Red blood cells carry oxygen to the working muscles. Oxygen is important for all activities but it is especially crucial for aerobic activities like marathons and endurance cycling events. Red blood cells also carry carbon dioxide away from the working muscles, where it is produced as a waste product. It is carried back to the lungs, where it is expelled from the body following gas exchange.

The double-circulatory network uses three types of **blood vessel** to carry blood: arteries, capillaries and veins. Each type of vessel has slightly different structural features. The reason for this is that each vessel carries blood at a different point in its journey and under different circumstances.

### Arteries

- **Arteries** carry blood away from the heart.

- Arteries carry oxygenated blood. The exception is the pulmonary artery, which carries deoxygenated blood.

- Blood pressure is high in the arteries and gets higher when exercise takes place.

- The blood travels at high speed in the arteries.

- The arteries have thick muscular walls and small **lumens**.

- The involuntary muscle in the walls of arteries is always under slight tension.

- When blood moves through arteries, it makes them pulse. As they retract to their normal diameter, blood is pushed along.

- During exercise, the arteries going to active muscles dilate. This means that they increase in diameter, allowing more oxygenated blood to be carried to working muscles.

- During exercise, the arteries going to inactive muscles and organs constrict. This means that they reduce in diameter and less blood is carried to inactive areas of the body, such as the digestive system, during exercise.

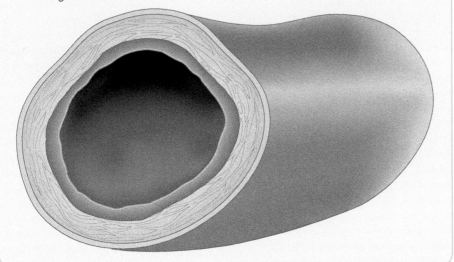

### Key terms

**Blood vessel:** A tubular structure that carries blood around our bodies.

**Arteries:** Blood vessels that carry oxygenated blood from the heart to muscles and organs.

**Lumen:** The internal diameter of a blood vessel.

### Study tip

The arteries, capillaries and veins are part of the vascular system. You can find out more about the short-term effects of exercise on the vascular system on pages 38–39 and more about the long-term effects of exercise on the vascular system on pages 43–45.

## Capillaries

- Capillaries look like a mesh wrapped around muscles and organs.

- There are lots of capillaries in every mesh.

- Each single capillary is very narrow. Blood cells have to travel through one at a time. This slows blood down.

- Each capillary has walls that are only one cell thick.

- Gases can diffuse through the walls of capillaries. Oxygen diffuses into muscles and organs through the capillaries. Carbon dioxide also diffuses into the blood through the capillaries. (See page 31 for more about diffusion.)

- Blood becomes deoxygenated at the capillaries.

- Capillaries are important during physical activity because they allow oxygen to enter the muscles through diffusion. Deoxygenated blood becomes oxygenated at the capillaries around the alveoli in the lungs.

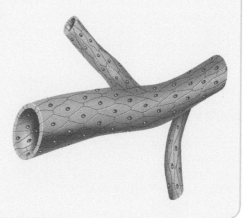

**Study tip**

During exercise more blood diffuses as it passes through the capillaries. This is explained in more detail on page 44.

**Key term**

**Capillaries:** Blood vessels that wrap around muscles and organs so that gas exchange can take place.

## Veins

- Veins carry blood back to the heart.

- Veins carry deoxygenated blood. The exception is the pulmonary vein, which carries oxygenated blood.

- Blood pressure is low in the veins.

- Blood travels at a fairly low speed in the veins.

- To prevent blood going in the wrong direction, veins have many one-way pocket valves.

- Veins have thinner walls than arteries.

- Veins have a larger lumen than arteries.

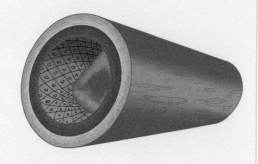

**Key term**

**Veins:** Blood vessels that carry deoxygenated blood from muscles and organs to the heart.

**Activity**

18 Using a soft modelling material, such as Plasticine or Play-Doh, model each of the three types of blood vessel, paying particular attention to the unique features of each vessel.

# Cardiac values

The volume of blood the heart pumps out depends on how much oxygen the working muscles and organs are demanding. The more oxygen they need, the more blood the heart pumps. This means the heart pumps more blood during exercise, as the working muscles demand more oxygen.

There are three values, called the cardiac values, which measure the volume of blood being pumped by the heart:

- **stroke volume** is the volume of blood pumped out of the heart to the body by the left ventricle during each contraction of the heart

- **heart rate** is the number of times the heart beats per minute

- **cardiac output** is the volume of blood pumped out of the heart per minute.

The heart can beat harder (raising stroke volume) and faster (raising heart rate), increasing the total volume of blood pumped out per minute (cardiac output).

The relationship of these three values can be expressed using the cardiac equation.

> The cardiac equation:
>
> stroke volume × heart rate = cardiac output

## Activity

19 Using a sponge ball to represent the heart, a bucket half full of water and an empty bucket, demonstrate heart rate, stroke volume and cardiac output. You may wish to do this outdoors.

a) Plunge the sponge ball into the bucket of water, so that it soaks up some of the water.

b) Hold the wet ball over the empty bucket and squeeze. The amount of water that comes out represents stroke volume, the amount of blood pumped out of the heart to the body by the left ventricle per beat.

c) Continue to do this for one minute, transferring water from one bucket to the other using the sponge. Each time you squeeze the ball, it represents one heartbeat. The total number of times you do it in a minute represents your heart rate.

d) At the end of the minute, the amount of water in the second bucket represents cardiac output, the amount of blood pumped out of the heart per minute.

e) Discuss what happens to stroke volume if you squeeze the ball harder or softer. What does this represent?

f) Discuss what happens to cardiac output if you squeeze the ball harder and more quickly. When and why would this happen in the body?

**Study tip**

This practical demonstration links very closely to the short-term effects of exercise on the heart, which is explored in more detail on pages 34–35.

# The pathway of air through the respiratory system

The respiratory system has two roles. Firstly, it brings oxygen into the body. Secondly, it expels carbon dioxide, a waste product that is created in the muscles when we exercise.

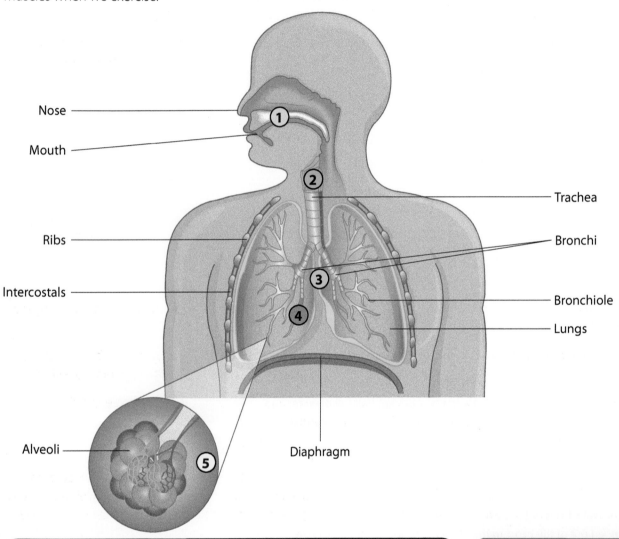

Nose

Mouth

Ribs

Intercostals

Alveoli

Trachea

Bronchi

Bronchiole

Lungs

Diaphragm

**The pathway of air through the respiratory system:**

1. Air enters the respiratory system through the nose and mouth.
2. Air travels down the trachea.
3. Air travels down the bronchi. 'Bronchi' is the plural of 'bronchus'.
4. Air travels down the narrower bronchioles.
5. Air reaches the alveoli where gas exchange will take place.

**Activity**

20  Create your own memory aid for remembering the pathway of air through the respiratory system. Consider using the first letter of each component and make a sentence out of words beginning with those letters.

▲  This diagram shows the structure of the respiratory system and the pathway of air through the respiratory system.

The intercostals are muscles that are located between the ribs. The diaphragm is a large muscle that sits below the lungs. Together, these muscles are called the respiratory muscles because they are responsible for the breathing process taking place.

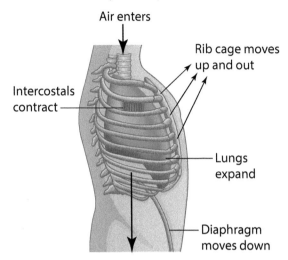

Air enters
Rib cage moves up and out
Intercostals contract
Lungs expand
Diaphragm moves down

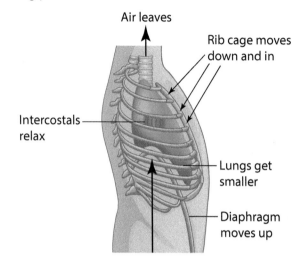

Air leaves
Rib cage moves down and in
Intercostals relax
Lungs get smaller
Diaphragm moves up

## Inhalation (breathing in)

1 The intercostals contract, pulling the ribs and lungs up and out.

2 The diaphragm contracts, pulling the bottom of the lungs down.

3 The thoracic cavity (the space inside the ribs) is now larger.

4 The lungs are stretched up, out and down, making the space inside them larger and reducing the air pressure inside them.

5 There is now a difference between the air pressure in the lungs and the air pressure outside the body. Air travels from areas of high pressure to areas of low pressure, so air is pulled into the lungs.

## Exhalation (breathing out)

1 The intercostals relax, returning the ribs and lungs to their original position.

2 The diaphragm relaxes, allowing the bottom of the lungs to move upwards to their original position.

3 The thoracic cavity (the space inside the ribs) is now smaller.

4 The lungs return to their resting size.

5 The air pressure outside the body is now lower than the air pressure inside the body. Air travels from areas of high pressure to areas of low pressure, so air leaves the lungs.

### Study tip

It is a common misunderstanding that the lungs work like a balloon. They do not. With a balloon, the air being blown in makes the balloon get bigger. The air pushes out the sides of the balloon. With the lungs, respiratory muscles actively pull out the chest, which stretches the lungs and pulls air in.

### Activity

21 Using the internet, find an animation of lungs inflating and deflating as a person inhales and exhales, or watch a person taking deep breaths. Describe what is happening as you watch. It might be useful to record your description on your phone, so you can listen to it again when you are revising.

# 1.1.17 Respiratory values

The volume of air breathed in and out by the lungs increases during exercise, to allow more oxygen to be brought into the body and more carbon dioxide to be expelled. There are three values, called the respiratory values, which measure the volume of air inhaled and exhaled:

- **tidal volume** is the volume of air inhaled or exhaled per breath; depth of breathing

- **breathing rate** is the number of breaths taken per minute

- **minute ventilation** is the volume of air inhaled or exhaled from the lungs per minute.

A person can breathe deeper (increasing tidal volume) and faster (increasing breathing rate), increasing the volume of air inhaled per minute (minute ventilation).

The relationship of these three values can be expressed using the respiratory equation.

> The respiratory equation:
>
> tidal volume × breathing rate = minute ventilation

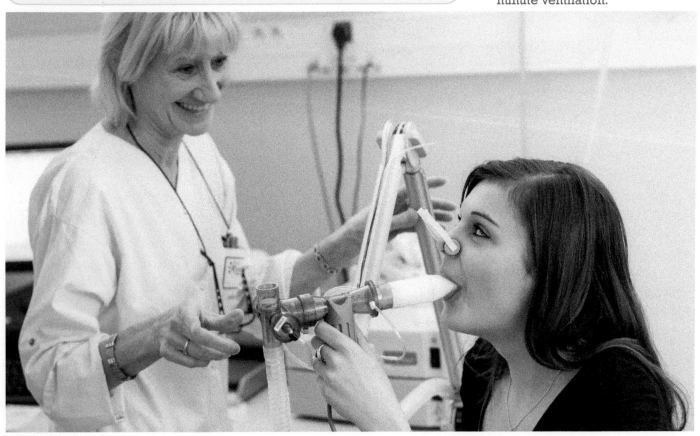

▼ A spirometer is a machine that measures lung volumes, including tidal volume, breathing rate and minute ventilation.

# Alveoli: the site of gas exchange

Once the alveoli in the lungs have filled with air, a process known as **gas exchange** takes place. Oxygen moves from the air in the alveoli into the blood in the capillaries, while carbon dioxide moves from the blood in the capillaries to the air in the alveoli. This is possible because the capillaries are wrapped tightly around the alveoli.

▼ This diagram shows how oxygen ($O_2$) and carbon dioxide ($CO_2$) exchange with one another in the alveoli.

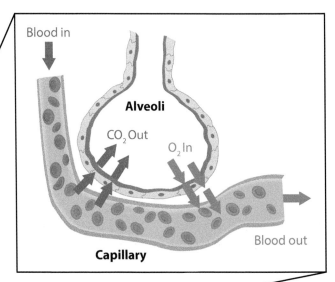

Blood in

**Alveoli**

$CO_2$ Out

$O_2$ In

Blood out

**Capillary**

Capillaries

Alveoli

## Diffusion

In order to understand gas exchange, you need to understand the process of **diffusion**. This is the term used to describe how gases move from an area of high **partial pressure** to an area of low partial pressure in an attempt to reach a balance.

Gas exchange is the diffusion of different gases in opposite directions at the same time: oxygen diffuses from the air in the alveoli into the blood in the capillaries at the same time as carbon dioxide from the blood in the capillaries diffuses into the air in the alveoli.

With moist, thin, single-cell thick walls, the alveoli are perfectly designed for diffusion, which allows the process of gas exchange to be very efficient.

### Key terms

**Gas exchange:** The movement of gases that takes place at the alveoli and capillaries.

**Diffusion:** The process of a gas moving from an area of high partial pressure to an area of low partial pressure.

**Partial pressure:** The pressure of a gas within a mixture of gases.

### Activity

22 Create a video presentation, or a storyboard for a video presentation, on gas exchange that could be shown to a class of Key Stage 3 students. You'll need to consider the best way to present the information. What is the simplest way to help someone understand it?

Your body requires **energy** to work. Whether you are taking a walk, stopping regularly for breaks, or sprinting 100 m as quickly as you can, your muscles require energy.

## Key terms

**Energy:** The capacity to do work.

**Intensity:** How hard you work.

**Duration:** How long an activity lasts.

◄ All types of activity require energy but the energy is released differently depending on the activity.

There are two methods that your muscles can use to release energy. The two methods used to release energy are:

- aerobic, using oxygen

- anaerobic, without oxygen.

Both of these methods are effective for releasing energy under the right circumstances but two factors determine which method is used:

- the **intensity** of the activity, how hard you work

- the **duration** of activity, how long the activity lasts for.

## Aerobic exercise

When a person works aerobically, they are able to release energy in the presence of oxygen, without **lactic acid** building up as a by-product. The fact that they are working at a low intensity allows oxygen to be delivered to the working muscles in time for it to be used and allows waste products, including lactic acid, to be carried away.

Releasing energy aerobically is the body's preferred way of working because lots of energy can be released using a relatively small amount of fuel. Consequently, people working aerobically can work for a long period of time.

▼ Marathon running is an example of aerobic exercise. It is performed at a relatively low intensity for a very long duration. The runners pace themselves by working at a low intensity in order to complete the race.

The fuel used to release energy when a person works aerobically is glucose or fats.

Examples of **aerobic exercise** include endurance cycling, long-distance swimming and marathon running.

## Anaerobic exercise

When the intensity of an activity is high, oxygen cannot be delivered to the working muscles and processed in time to be used. As a result, the body has to work without oxygen; it works anaerobically. This does not mean that a person is not breathing. It simply means that the muscular contractions are happening too rapidly for oxygen to be delivered in time for it to be used.

Lactic acid is a by-product of anaerobic energy release. Although lactic acid does not build up quickly enough in the working muscles to impact an activity that has a very short duration – such as a triple jump – it will certainly affect performance at the end of a sprint race.

Examples of **anaerobic exercise** include sprinting, throwing and jumping events.

◀ Sprinting is an example of anaerobic exercise because it is performed at a very high intensity for a short duration. Such intensity cannot be maintained for a long duration.

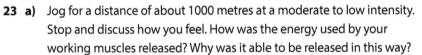

## Activity

**23 a)** Jog for a distance of about 1000 metres at a moderate to low intensity. Stop and discuss how you feel. How was the energy used by your working muscles released? Why was it able to be released in this way?

**b)** Sprint as far as you can. (The furthest anyone will get will probably be 200 metres.) What starts to happen in your legs the further you go? Can you explain this?

**24 a)** Write down a list of ten sporting activities and add the relative intensity and duration alongside each one.

**b)** Place each sporting activity on a continuum, with the most aerobic at one end, and the most anaerobic at the other. You may need to debate the exact position of some in the middle. Remember that the intensity and duration of each activity are the two things to think about when considering where they should go on the continuum.

# The short-term effects of exercise

During exercise, muscles require more oxygen if they are going to work aerobically. They also produce more waste products, including carbon dioxide and lactic acid, as well as heat. Therefore, for the body to continue to function as efficiently as possible – for more oxygen to be delivered to the working muscles and for waste products to be removed – changes take place to four key body systems:

- the cardiac system
- the respiratory system
- the muscular system
- the vascular system.

## The short-term effects of exercise on the cardiac system

In order to meet the increased demand for oxygen during exercise, more oxygenated blood must be delivered to the working muscles by the heart. This means that cardiac output must increase. Cardiac output increases when stroke volume and heart rate increase.

These three graphs show how stroke volume, heart rate and cardiac output are affected by exercise:

▲ There are many short-term effects of exercise that impact on a sportsperson as they perform.

### The short-term effect of exercise on stroke volume

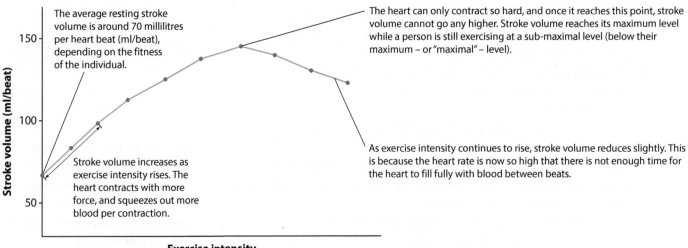

The average resting stroke volume is around 70 millilitres per heart beat (ml/beat), depending on the fitness of the individual.

Stroke volume increases as exercise intensity rises. The heart contracts with more force, and squeezes out more blood per contraction.

The heart can only contract so hard, and once it reaches this point, stroke volume cannot go any higher. Stroke volume reaches its maximum level while a person is still exercising at a sub-maximal level (below their maximum – or "maximal" – level).

As exercise intensity continues to rise, stroke volume reduces slightly. This is because the heart rate is now so high that there is not enough time for the heart to fill fully with blood between beats.

# The short-term effect of exercise on heart rate

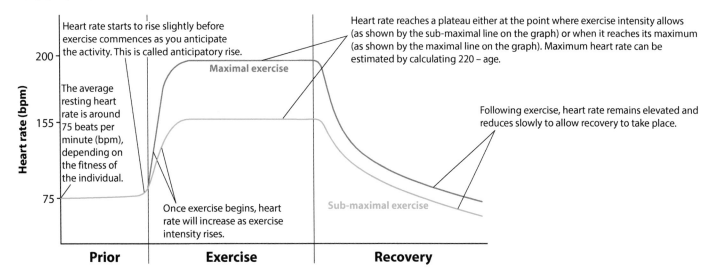

Heart rate starts to rise slightly before exercise commences as you anticipate the activity. This is called anticipatory rise.

The average resting heart rate is around 75 beats per minute (bpm), depending on the fitness of the individual.

Maximal exercise

Heart rate reaches a plateau either at the point where exercise intensity allows (as shown by the sub-maximal line on the graph) or when it reaches its maximum (as shown by the maximal line on the graph). Maximum heart rate can be estimated by calculating 220 – age.

Following exercise, heart rate remains elevated and reduces slowly to allow recovery to take place.

Once exercise begins, heart rate will increase as exercise intensity rises.

Sub-maximal exercise

Heart rate (bpm) — 200, 155, 75

Prior | Exercise | Recovery

# The short-term effect of exercise on cardiac output

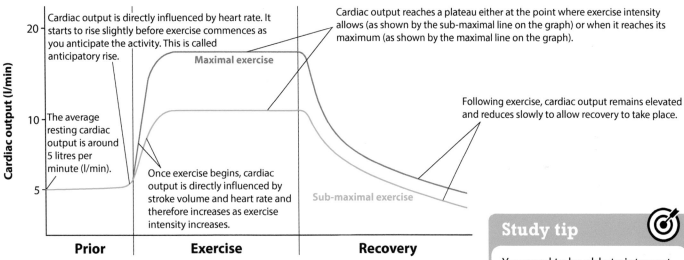

Cardiac output is directly influenced by heart rate. It starts to rise slightly before exercise commences as you anticipate the activity. This is called anticipatory rise.

Maximal exercise

Cardiac output reaches a plateau either at the point where exercise intensity allows (as shown by the sub-maximal line on the graph) or when it reaches its maximum (as shown by the maximal line on the graph).

Following exercise, cardiac output remains elevated and reduces slowly to allow recovery to take place.

The average resting cardiac output is around 5 litres per minute (l/min).

Once exercise begins, cardiac output is directly influenced by stroke volume and heart rate and therefore increases as exercise intensity increases.

Sub-maximal exercise

Cardiac output (l/min) — 20, 10, 5

Prior | Exercise | Recovery

## Activity

**25 a)** In a state of rest, find your pulse at either the carotid artery (in your neck) or the radial artery (in your wrist) and count how many times your heart beats in one minute.

**b)** Take part in some vigorous activity, stopping at regular intervals to measure your heart rate (pulse).

**c)** Record the information collected for a) and b) in a table before plotting it on a graph. Does your graph look like the heart rate graph above?

**d)** Work with a partner to extend this activity and create different graphs. One of you could work continuously, which may allow you to see a plateau, while the other could work in an interval style, which would show you how heart rate responds to exercise intensity.

**e)** Compare your graphs with others and analyse the results.

**f)** What have you learned from your analysis? What conclusion can you draw?

## Study tip

You need to be able to interpret data relating to short-term effects of exercise. Note what is on the *x* and *y* axes, and the scale that each graph uses. Also, when a line on a graph flattens out, it is said to 'plateau'.

## Study tip

This information on the short-term effects of exercise on the cardiac system is closely linked to the information on the volume of blood pumped from the heart on page 27.

# The short-term effects of exercise on the respiratory system

The respiratory system must bring more oxygen into the body during exercise, to meet the increased demand for oxygen from the working muscles.

When breathing rate and tidal volume increase, minute ventilation increases. This means that more oxygen is brought into the body during exercise than during rest.

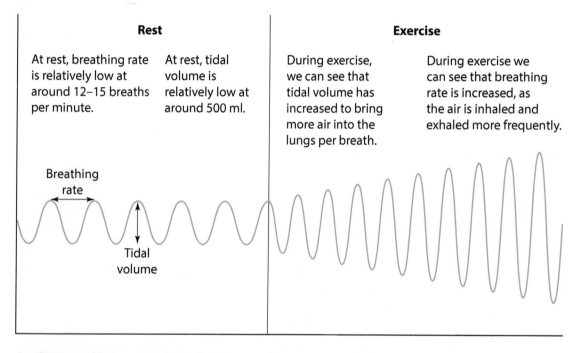

**Rest**

At rest, breathing rate is relatively low at around 12–15 breaths per minute.

At rest, tidal volume is relatively low at around 500 ml.

**Exercise**

During exercise, we can see that tidal volume has increased to bring more air into the lungs per breath.

During exercise we can see that breathing rate is increased, as the air is inhaled and exhaled more frequently.

▲ On page 30 you were introduced to a spirometer, which is a machine that measures lung volumes. This is a spirometer trace. It shows the changes that take place when a person moves from rest to exercise.

**Activity**

26 **a)** Using the spirometer trace as a guide, explain what happens to the breathing rate and tidal volume when a person moves from rest to exercise.

**b)** Add a sporting example, explaining when a person's breathing rate and tidal volume increase and decrease during a performance.

27 Can you see any similarities between short-term effects of exercise on the respiratory system and short-term effects of exercise on the cardiac system?

**Study tip**

This information on the short-term effects of exercise on the respiratory system is closely linked to the information on the volume of air being breathed in and out of the lungs on page 30.

## The short-term effects of exercise on the muscular system

### Increase in muscle temperature

During exercise, muscles create heat and the temperature of the muscles increases as a result. This increase in temperature has benefits. It increases the pliability of muscles, increasing the speed and strength of contractions and reducing the risk of a muscle strain.

### Lactic acid production

Lactic acid is produced as a by-product of anaerobic exercise. A build-up of lactic acid results in muscle fatigue, which is a reduction in the muscle's ability to produce force. This brings pain and, sometimes, cramp, both of which negatively impact sporting performance.

▲ Sweating is one indication that muscle temperature is rising. By releasing sweat, the body is able to control its core temperature and prevent overheating. Overheating can cause nausea, dizziness and feelings of fatigue.

◀ Muscular fatigue has an impact on a sportsperson, who experiences pain and reduced performance as a result.

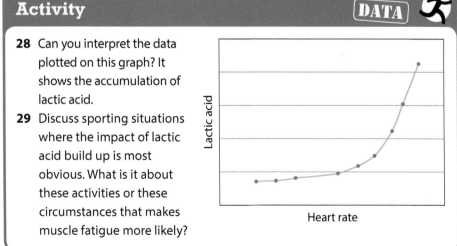

**Activity**    DATA

28 Can you interpret the data plotted on this graph? It shows the accumulation of lactic acid.

29 Discuss sporting situations where the impact of lactic acid build up is most obvious. What is it about these activities or these circumstances that makes muscle fatigue more likely?

# The short-term effects of exercise on the vascular system

During exercise, it is not only necessary to breathe in more air and pump oxygenated blood more quickly, it is also important to circulate the blood to the working muscles so that the oxygen is delivered to where it is needed most.

## The redistribution of blood flow during physical activity

When exercise begins, the body alters its priorities because it needs to deliver more oxygen to the working muscles. While at rest, a high proportion of blood is directed towards the organs, but during exercise the majority of blood is re-directed towards the working muscles. This increases oxygen delivery to the working muscles. For example, oxygenated blood is directed away from the digestive system and towards the quadriceps and hamstrings.

The **vascular shunt mechanism** is the process used to redistribute oxygenated blood when exercise begins. It is achieved by vasoconstriction and vasodilation, which is altering the size of the artery lumens supplying different areas of the body.

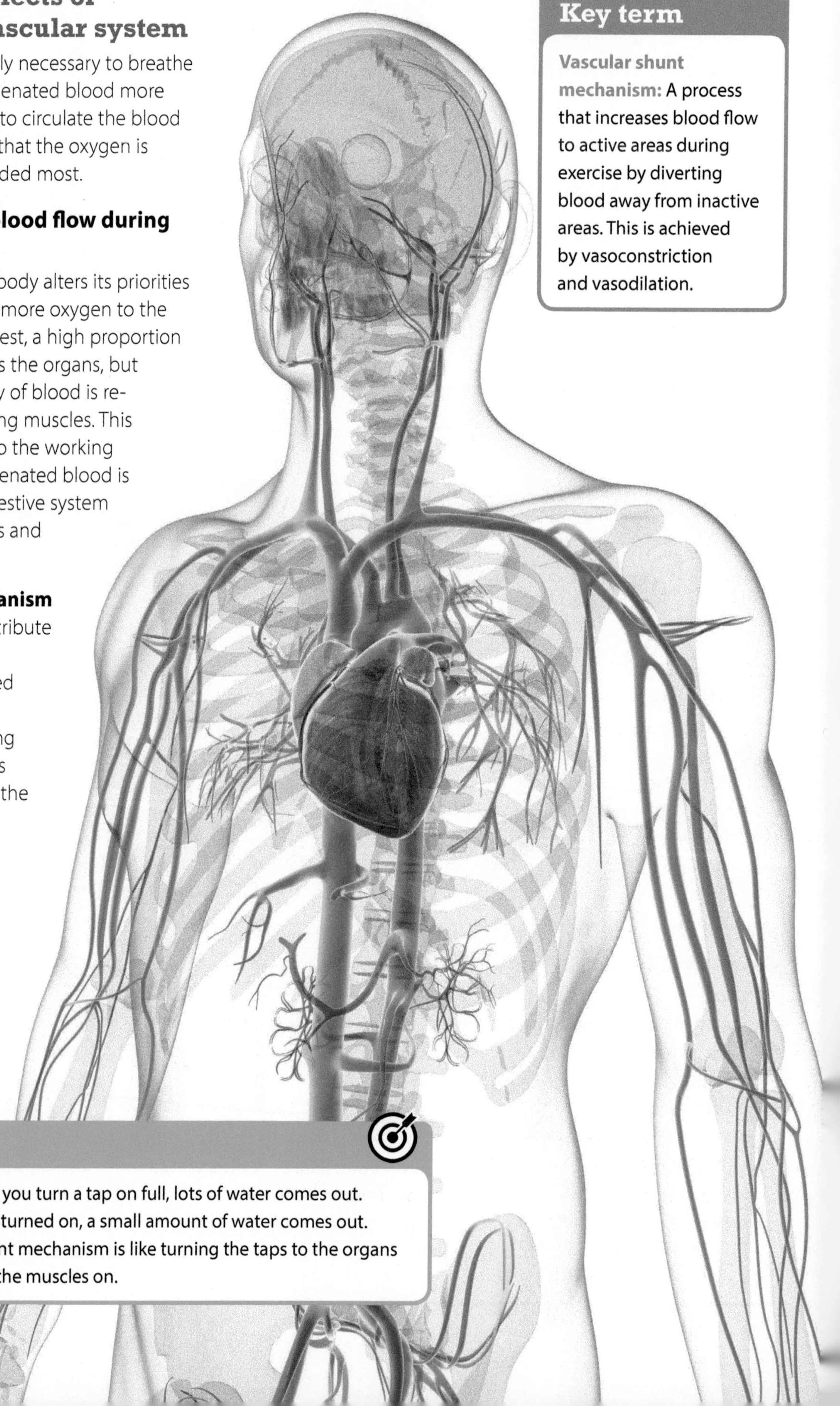

**Key term**

**Vascular shunt mechanism:** A process that increases blood flow to active areas during exercise by diverting blood away from inactive areas. This is achieved by vasoconstriction and vasodilation.

**Study tip**

Think of arteries like taps. If you turn a tap on full, lots of water comes out. When a tap is only partially turned on, a small amount of water comes out. Triggering the vascular shunt mechanism is like turning the taps to the organs off and turning the taps to the muscles on.

## Vasoconstriction

**Vasoconstriction** is the narrowing of the internal diameter (lumen) of a blood vessel to restrict the volume of blood travelling through it. The arteries constrict during exercise so that less blood is delivered to inactive areas, such as the digestive system.

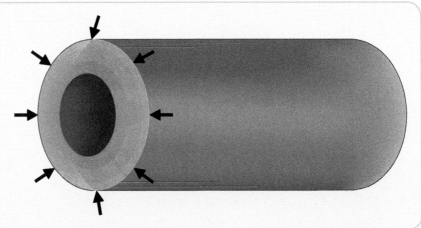

## Normal vascular tone

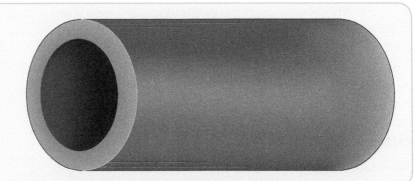

## Vasodilation

**Vasodilation** is the widening of the lumen of a blood vessel to increase the volume of blood travelling through it. The arteries dilate during exercise so that more blood is delivered to active areas, increasing their oxygen supply.

Without the vascular shunt mechanism redistributing blood during exercise you would find taking part in sport unsustainable. Your muscles would be forced to work anaerobically and this would lead to muscle fatigue.

## Activity

30 Write down all the key phrases relating to the vascular shunt mechanism on a piece of paper. Include 'arteries', 'vasoconstriction', etc. Now attempt to explain the process to a partner without using any of these terms. You'll need to be very creative with your vocabulary! Once you've done that, write an explanation of vascular shunting using all the phrases and terms, which should be much easier.

## Key terms

**Vasoconstriction:** The narrowing of the internal diameter (lumen) of a blood vessel to decrease blood flow.

**Vasodilation:** The widening of the internal diameter (lumen) of a blood vessel to increase blood flow.

# The long-term training effects of exercise

Regular effective training has significant long-term effects on all of the body's systems. Positive **adaptations** take place as a result of training, improving the efficiency of the body's systems. These adaptations ensure the performer is better able to cope with the demands of the activity and, as a result, they will perform better over time.

Athletes will train to develop the components of fitness that are most important for their activity and the long-term effects of exercise on individual athletes will vary as a result. Adaptations can, however, be divided into two broad categories: the long-term effects of exercise on the **musculo-skeletal system** and the long-term effect of exercise on the **cardiovascular-respiratory system**.

## The long-term effects of exercise on the musculo-skeletal system

There are three adaptations to the musculo-skeletal system that take place as a result of regular exercise.

### Increased bone density

Training and competing in high-impact sports stresses the bones and joints. This results in increased **bone density** over time. Bones become thicker and stronger, as a result of increased calcium deposits, which means that fractures are less likely to occur.

▲ Gymnasts develop higher bone density because of the stress put through their bones as a result of the high-impact nature of their sport.

**Study tip**

The components of fitness (pages 48–62), the principles of training (pages 63–67) and the long-term training effects of exercise all link together.

**Key terms**

**Adaptation:** A physical change that makes a body system more efficient.

**Musculo-skeletal system:** The name given to the combined body system that involves the muscular system and the skeletal system.

**Cardiovascular-respiratory system:** The name given to the combined body system that involves your cardiac, vascular and respiratory systems. These are usually combined when discussing oxygen delivery.

**Bone density:** The thickness and strength of bones.

## Hypertrophy of muscle and increased muscular strength

Performers who place strength demands on their muscles will see them develop in size over time. This process is called **hypertrophy**. During strength training, muscle fibres develop micro-tears as a result of the stress placed on them. As these tears heal, the muscle fibres grow and develop, which makes the muscle larger and stronger. Trained muscles are also capable of faster contractions, increasing a performer's speed and power.

◀ Sprint kayakers require a lot of **muscular strength** in their upper body in order to overcome the resistance of the water.

### Activity

DATA

31 The table shows a person's 1 Repetition Maximum for three different exercises before and after they took part in a weight training programme.

| Exercise | Before | After |
|---|---|---|
| Bicep curl | 10 kg | 15 kg |
| Shoulder press | 40 kg | 60 kg |
| Leg press | 50 kg | 80 kg |

   a) For which exercise did the person experience the greatest increase in strength?

   b) What increase in strength did the person experience for the exercise with the lowest increase in strength?

   c) Present the information in the table as a line graph.

### Increase muscular endurance and increased resistance to fatigue

**Muscular endurance** is the ability to contract your muscles repeatedly without fatigue. It is critical for performers who need their muscles to perform over an extended period of time and endurance athletes will, therefore, train to increase their muscular endurance. Having high levels of muscular endurance means that their bodies are able to receive and use oxygen very efficiently. It means they are able to work aerobically at higher intensities for longer. They have a higher anaerobic threshold, delaying the point at which lactic acid is produced as a by-product. These factors, combined with increased tolerance to any lactic acid produced, increases their ability to resist fatigue.

▼ Endurance swimmers, like Keri-anne Payne, are not as muscular as swimmers who compete over short distances. This is because endurance training encourages high levels of muscular endurance and resistance to fatigue rather than hypertrophy and muscular strength.

**Study tip**

Training thresholds are discussed on pages 69–73.

**Key term**

Muscular endurance: The ability to move your body and contract your muscles repeatedly without fatigue.

**Activity**

**32 a)** Draw up a list of ten different sports.

**b)** Decide whether people taking part in each sport need more muscular strength or more muscular endurance to succeed. Organise the sports into three groups: those that need more muscular strength for success, those that need more muscular endurance for success and those that need both for success.

**c)** Discuss how the requirements of each sport might influence a performer's training.

# The long-term effects of exercise on the cardiovascular-respiratory system

Training and competing in activities that are mainly aerobic will, over time, bring adaptations to the cardiovascular-respiratory system.

## Cardiac hypertrophy

As a result of cardiovascular endurance training, the heart experiences hypertrophy. The walls of the heart become more muscular and the heart becomes more efficient.

Cardiac hypertrophy allows the heart to pump more blood out per beat, increasing stroke volume when the body is at rest. As a result, resting heart rate decreases because the heart does not need to beat as fast to deliver enough blood to the muscles and organs. Higher stroke volume also increases cardiac output, because more blood leaves the heart each minute when a person is exercising. This brings improved aerobic performance.

Compared to an untrained person, a trained person will have:

- higher stroke volume
- lower resting heart rate
- higher cardiac output when exercising.

**Study tip**

Look back at page 27 to remind yourself about the cardiac values.

## Activity DATA

33 This graph shows a person's resting heart rate before and after they took part in a training programme to improve their cardiovascular endurance.

**Resting heart rate**

(Graph: y-axis "Beats per minute (bpm)" from 0 to 80; x-axis "Training programme" with categories "Before" and "After"; the bar declines from about 70 before to about 50 after.)

a) What was the person's resting heart rate before they took part in the training programme?

b) By how many beats per minute does the person's resting heart rate reduce as a result of the training programme?

c) Explain why the person's resting heart rate reduces as a result of the training programme.

▶ As highly trained aerobic athletes, the Brownlee brothers, who compete in international triathlons, both benefit from cardiac hypertrophy. The image on the left shows a normal heart, the image on the right shows a heart with increased muscle brought about by cardiac hypertrophy.

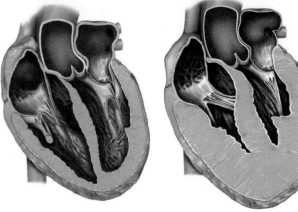

## Increased strength of respiratory muscles

Endurance training increases the strength of a performer's respiratory muscles.

As the intercostals and the diaphragm get stronger, they are able to stretch the lungs up, out and down more, increasing tidal volume (the volume of air inhaled or exhaled with each breath) and minute ventilation (the volume of air inhaled or exhaled from the lungs per minute) during exercise.

Compared to an untrained person, a trained person will have:

- higher tidal volume during exercise
- higher minute ventilation during exercise.

> **Study tip**
>
> Remind yourself of the role that respiratory muscles play in breathing on page 29 and the respiratory values on page 30.

▲ With highly developed respiratory muscles and huge lung capacity, distance swimmers are able to bring far more oxygen into their bodies than untrained people.

## Capilliarisation

A trained endurance athlete will see an increase in the number of capillaries that wrap around their alveoli and muscles. This is called **capilliarisation**. As a result of capilliarisation, more gas exchange takes place, increasing the speed at which both oxygen delivery and carbon dioxide removal takes place.

> **Key term**
>
> Capilliarisation: An increase in the number of blood capillaries in the body. It is one of the long-term effects of exercise.

## Increased aerobic capacity and rate of recovery

As a result of the numerous cardiovascular-respiratory adaptations discussed, an improvement in overall aerobic capacity and rate of recovery is also a long-term effect of exercise.

## Increased aerobic capacity

An athlete's **aerobic capacity** is their ability to take in oxygen and use it for aerobic work. The higher a person's aerobic capacity, the harder they are able to work while still performing aerobically. This means that they can perform at higher intensity before they need to start releasing energy anaerobically. The effect of this is that they can work for longer before the effects of fatigue take hold.

Elite long-distance rowers, endurance cyclists, long-distance swimmers and marathon runners all have huge aerobic capacities.

## Faster rate of recovery

Following exercise, the rate that an athlete recovers tells you a lot about their aerobic fitness. Full recovery will see cardiac and respiratory values return to resting levels. As a result of high stroke volume and high tidal volume, trained athletes will recover far quicker than untrained people.

### Key terms

**Aerobic capacity:** The greatest volume of oxygen that can be consumed and used by a person.

**Rate of recovery:** The speed at which the body returns back to normal after exercise.

### Study tip

Collection and use of data measuring the long-term effects of exercise links to the development of the components of fitness, which are discussed on pages 48–62.

◀ While trained endurance athletes will be exhausted following a race because of the huge effort they put in, their **rate of recovery** will be very quick once they have finished, as shown in the heart rate graph below. This is because their bodies are so efficient at delivering oxygen and removing waste products.

### Activity

**34** Create an A3 revision sheet or mind map that details all the long-term (training) effects of exercise.

# Practice questions

**1** Which **one** of the following is an articulating bone at the shoulder joint?
Put a tick (✔) in the box next to the correct answer.
A  Femur ☐
B  Phalanges ☐
C  Ulna ☐
D  Humerus ☑
**[1]**

**2** Which **one** of the following is **not** a blood vessel attached to the heart?
Put a tick (✔) in the box next to the correct answer.
A  Pulmonary vein ☐
B  Ventricle ☑
C  Vena cava ☐
D  Aorta ☐
**[1]**

**3** Which **one** of the following is the best example of aerobic exercise?
Put a tick (✔) in the box next to the correct answer.
A  Cycling 1000 m ☐
B  Running a marathon ☑
C  Throwing a discus ☐
D  Playing a football match ☐
**[1]**

**4** Which **one** of the following statements is false?
Put a tick (✔) in the box next to the correct answer.
✗A  A cartwheel takes place in the frontal plane. ☐
✗B  A pirouette rotates around the longitudinal axis. ☐
Ⓒ  A tucked front somersault rotates around the frontal axis. ☑
D  An axis is an imaginary line that a movement rotates around. ☐
**[1]**

**5** Explain the role of ligaments at a joint. **[2]**
to join bone to bone at any joint

**6** Explain two roles muscles can play during movement. agonist → contracting **[4]**
antagonist → relaxing

**7** Compare the structure and function of an artery and a vein. artery : thick **[4]**
vein : valves     muscular
  thin walls     walls
  large lumen    small lumen
(deox to heart)  (ox away from heart)

**8** Figure 1 shows a diagram of the shoulder. Label bone **A** and muscle **B**.

A ___humerus___

B ___pectorals___

▲ **Figure 1** **[2]**

**9** Describe the potential long-term effects of exercise on the musculo-skeletal system? Why do different sports performers experience different long-term effects on the musculo-skeletal system? **[6]**

**10** Using practical examples, describe how different classes of lever are used in sporting performance. How are some levers more beneficial than others? **[6]**

When you have worked through this chapter, you will have developed knowledge and understanding of:

- the components of fitness

- the principles of training

- how to optimise training

- how to prevent injury.

**Fitness** is your ability to meet the physical demands placed on you by the environment. Fitness is a general term, but it can be broken down into ten components of fitness.

## The ten components of fitness

Each component of fitness describes a specific aspect of sporting performance. Performance in different sports requires a different balance of these components. Some sports need performers to develop a high level of fitness in just one or two components, while other sports, including games activities, require performers to develop a high level of fitness in many different components in order to excel.

**Activity**

1    Make your own collage of the components of fitness. Choose images that clearly represent each component of fitness. Look at the definitions of each component of fitness in the glossary to help you.

**Study tip**

If you can remember 'Fitness Components Are Required Because Many Sportspeople Can't Perform Superbly', then you have a memory aid to recall the ten components of fitness.

Fitness testing is used to measure a performer's level of fitness in one or more of the ten components of fitness. When a performer knows which components of fitness are most important for their sport, and what their level of fitness is in each of these components, they can design a training programme that suits their specific needs.

When you carry out fitness testing you collect a lot of data.

**DATA**

## Types of data

Data can be **quantitative** or **qualitative**.

When carrying out fitness tests, the data generated will be quantitative. Quantitative data focuses on measuring things, and involves numbers. And, because it is based on facts, it gives you objective answers to your questions.

Qualitative data focuses on gaining a deeper understanding of issues and gathers data about people's thoughts and opinions. It, therefore, gives you more subjective answers to your questions.

## Presenting quantitative data

Quantitative data can be presented in tables, as bar charts, line graphs and pie charts. Presenting quantitative data visually makes it easier to analyse.

### Activity **DATA**

**2** Analyse the pie charts. What do they tell you about the agility of this year group?

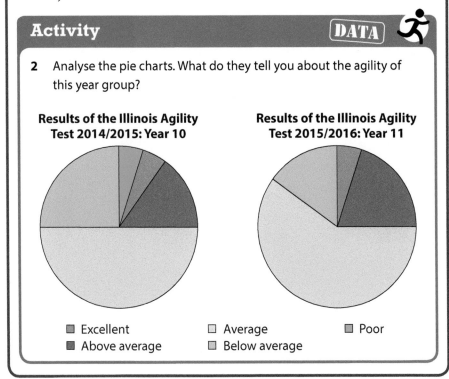

**Results of the Illinois Agility Test 2014/2015: Year 10**

**Results of the Illinois Agility Test 2015/2016: Year 11**

☐ Excellent  ☐ Average  ☐ Poor
☐ Above average  ☐ Below average

### Key terms

**Quantitative data:** Data that measures things and involves numbers. Quantitative data gives you an objective answer to your question.

**Qualitative data:** Data that focuses on gaining a deeper understanding of people's thoughts and opinions. Qualitative data gives you a subjective answer to your question.

**Normative data:** Normative data shows the results for 'normal' people. Data is collected from a large sample of people and the most common results are established.

### Activity **DATA**

**3 a)** Carry out each of the fitness tests described on pages 50–62.

**b)** Record your results in a table, using appropriate units of measurement. It is helpful to have all your results together.

**c)** Compare the quantitative data you have collected with the **normative data** provided on pages 50–62.

**d)** Choose one fitness test and create a pie chart, a line graph or a bar graph showing the results collected by your whole class.

**e)** Analyse the quantitative data you have collected. What conclusions can you draw? Which components of fitness are you strongest in and which components of fitness are you weakest in?

# 1.2.3 Cardiovascular endurance

**Cardiovascular endurance**, which is also referred to as stamina, is the ability of the cardiovascular system to deliver oxygenated blood to the working muscles and to remove waste products, such as carbon dioxide and lactic acid. It is, in other words, a measure of the body's ability to release energy aerobically.

Cardiovascular endurance is particularly important for activities that take place over an extended period of time, including marathon running, endurance cycling, long-distance swimming and long-distance rowing.

## Testing cardiovascular endurance

There are two fitness tests for measuring cardiovascular endurance:

1   Cooper 12-minute run/walk test

2   Multi-stage fitness test.

> ### Key term
>
> **Cardiovascular endurance:** The ability to release energy aerobically over a long period of time. It is also referred to as stamina.

▲ Elite marathon running, because of its long duration (it takes over two hours to run the 26 miles 385 yards of a marathon), is an excellent example of a sport requiring cardiovascular endurance.

## Cooper 12-minute run/walk test

**Objective:** Run or walk continuously for 12 minutes, travelling as far as you can in that time.

**Protocol:**

1 Conduct a suitable warm up, if necessary.

2 Use a 400 metre running track.

3 Start a stopwatch at the beginning of the test. Count the number of laps and part laps you complete in 12 minutes.

4 Calculate how many metres you travelled. Round down to the nearest metre.

▼ Normative data for 15–16-year-olds for the Cooper 12-minute run/walk test.

|  | **Male** | **Female** |
|---|---|---|
| **Excellent** | > 2800 m | > 2100 m |
| **Above average** | 2500–2800 m | 2000–2100 m |
| **Average** | 2300–2499 m | 1700–1999 m |
| **Below average** | 2200–2299 m | 1600–1699 m |
| **Poor** | < 2200 m | < 1600 m |

*Source: Brian Mac Sports Coach, www.brianmac.co.uk*

**Study tip**

- > means 'more than'
- < means 'less than'

These symbols are often used in normative data tables.

## Multi-stage fitness test

**Objective:** Run 20-metre shuttles, keeping up with bleeps, which get closer together as the test progresses.

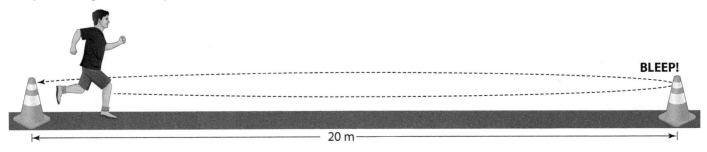

BLEEP!

20 m

**Protocol:**

1 Conduct a suitable warm up, if necessary.

2 Set out marker cones 20 metres apart.

3 Use a multi-stage fitness test recording. Start the recording when everyone is ready.

4 Run 20-metre shuttles, ensuring you arrive at the marker cone before or as the recording bleeps. If you reach the marker cone before the bleep, wait until the bleep has sounded before turning and running the next shuttle.

5 As the bleeps get closer together through the test, you will need to work harder. If you fail to reach the marker cone before the bleep on two consecutive occasions, you will be asked to stop and record the level you last completed properly.

▼ Normative data for 15–16-year-olds for the multi-stage fitness test.

|  | **Male** | **Female** |
|---|---|---|
| Excellent | Level 12 | Level 10 |
| Above average | Level 11 | Level 9 |
| Average | Level 8 | Level 6 |
| Below average | Level 7 | Level 5 |
| Poor | < Level 6 | < Level 4 |

*Source: Brian Mac Sports Coach, www.brianmac.co.uk*

# 1.2.4 Muscular endurance

**Muscular endurance** is a measure of how long a performer's muscles can contract repeatedly before they suffer muscular fatigue. It relies on the body's ability to deliver oxygen and remove lactic acid efficiently. This component of fitness is especially important for endurance athletes such as rowers, cyclists and runners, and is also needed by games players.

◀ Muscular endurance is particularly important for all activities where performance relies on repeated muscular contraction over an extended duration.

## Testing muscular endurance

There are two fitness tests for measuring cardiovascular endurance:

1 Sit-up test

2 Press-up test.

**Objective:** Perform as many sit-ups or press-ups as you can in one minute.

**Protocol:**

The protocol for both tests is the same.

1 Conduct a suitable warm up, if necessary.

2 Ensure you know the correct technique for a sit-up, a full press-up or a modified press-up.

3 Establish the correct start position, on an appropriate surface.

4 Start a stop watch and count how many successful repetitions you can complete in one minute. Resting is only allowed in the start position.

| | Exercise start position | Exercise finish position |
|---|---|---|
| Sit-up |  | |

▼ Normative data for 16–19-year-olds for the sit-up test.

| | Excellent | Above average | Average | Below average | Poor |
|---|---|---|---|---|---|
| Male | > 30 | 26–30 | 20–25 | 17–19 | < 17 |
| Female | > 25 | 21–25 | 15–20 | 9–14 | < 9 |

*Source: Davis, B. et al.* Physical Education and the Study of Sport, 4th edn., *Mosby Publishing, 2000.*

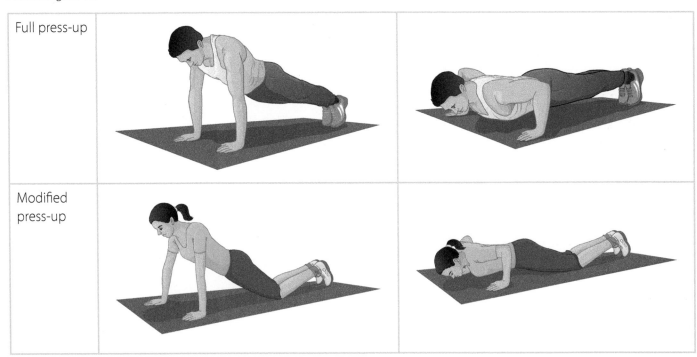

| Full press-up | |
|---|---|
| Modified press-up | |

▼ Normative data for 17–19-year-olds for the press-up test.

| | Excellent | Good | Above average | Average | Below average | Poor | Very poor |
|---|---|---|---|---|---|---|---|
| Full press-up | > 56 | 47–56 | 35–46 | 19–34 | 11–18 | 4–10 | < 4 |
| Modified press-up | > 35 | 28–35 | 21–27 | 11–20 | 6–10 | 2–5 | 0–1 |

*Data: Golding, L.A. et al.* The Y's Way to Physical Fitness, 3rd edn. *Human Kinetics Publishers, 1986.*

**Speed** is the rate at which an individual is able to perform a movement, or cover a distance. Speed is crucial in many sports, whether throwing a fast punch in boxing, sprinting towards the try line in rugby, performing a fast break in basketball or competing in a 100 m race.

> **Key term**
>
> **Speed:** The ability to move quickly across the ground, or to move your limbs rapidly through movements.

◀ Speed is generally associated with sprinting because the more speed someone has, the quicker they can cover the ground. However, performing a sporting action at high speed is important for many activities. For example, in boxing, throwing a punch at high speed gives your opponent less chance to react and avoid it.

## Testing speed: 30-metre sprint test

**Objective:** Sprint a 30-metre distance as quickly as possible, given a flying start.

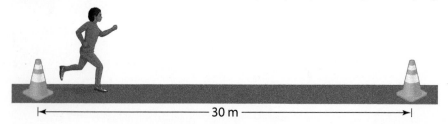

**Protocol:**

1 Conduct a suitable warm up, if necessary.

2 Select a suitable sprinting area, about 70–80 metres long.

3 Mark a distance of 30 metres, using two marker cones, near the middle of the sprinting area.

4 Accelerate towards the first cone, so that you are running at your maximum speed as you pass it. Continue running, as fast as you can, past the second cone.

5 A stopwatch is started as you pass the first cone and stopped as you pass the second cone. The time is recorded to one decimal place.

▼ Normative data for 16–19-year-olds for the 30-metre sprint test.

|  | **Male** | **Female** |
|---|---|---|
| Excellent | < 4 seconds | < 4.5 seconds |
| Above average | 4.2–4 seconds | 4.6–4.5 seconds |
| Average | 4.4–4.3 seconds | 4.8–4.7 seconds |
| Below average | 4.6–4.5 seconds | 5–4.9 seconds |
| Poor | > 4.6 seconds | > 5 seconds |

*Source: Davis, B. et al. Physical Education and the Study of Sport, 4th edn., Mosby Publishing, 2000.*

**Strength** is the amount of force that muscles can generate to overcome resistance. The stronger you are, the easier it is to perform everyday tasks like lifting and carrying. In sport, strength can be used to lift a weight, hold your body in a given position or to overcome an opponent.

### Key term

**Strength:** The maximum force a muscle or a group of muscles can apply against resistance.

▼ Whether lifting a weight, like in weightlifting, or your own body, like in rock climbing, strength is important for many different types of activity.

## Testing strength

There are two fitness tests for measuring strength:

1   Grip strength dynamometer test

2   1 Repetition Maximum (RM)

## Grip strength dynamometer test

**Objective:** Generate the highest possible force reading on the grip dynamometer to measure grip strength.

**Protocol:**

**1** Use a grip dynamometer.

**2** Record the highest reading from three attempts, using your dominant hand and allowing a one-minute rest between attempts.

**3** Grip strength is usually measured in kilograms (kg).

▼ Normative data for 16–19-year-olds for the grip strength dynamometer test.

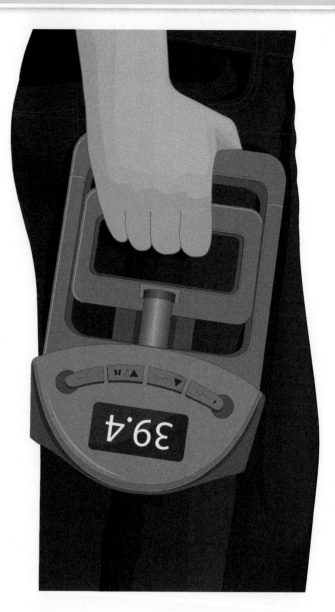

|  | Male | Female |
|---|---|---|
| Excellent | > 56 kg | > 36 kg |
| Above average | 51–56 kg | 31–36 kg |
| Average | 45–50 kg | 25–30 kg |
| Below average | 39–44 kg | 19–24 kg |
| Poor | 39 kg | < 19 kg |

*Source: Davis, B. et al. Physical Education and the Study of Sport, 4th edn., Mosby Publishing, 2000.*

## 1 Repetition Maximum (RM)

**Objective:** Using a suitable exercise to test the muscle group chosen, lift the heaviest possible weight, once.

**Protocol:**

**1** Conduct a suitable warm up, if necessary.

**2** Select the muscle group you would like to test.

**3** Select an appropriate exercise. For example, you can test lower body strength using a squat exercise.

**4** Select a realistic, achievable weight to lift and lift the weight once, using the correct technique.

**5** After a rest of several minutes, increase the weight and lift again.

**6** Continue increasing the weight until you cannot lift it. The last weight you are able to lift is your 1 Repetition Maximum, or your 1RM.

**7** Find normative data for the exercise you chose.

**Power** is the ability to combine strength and speed.

The ability to contract muscles quickly, with great strength, is used in sport to power out of the blocks and through the drive phase in a sprint race, to hit a ball with great power in golf and racket sports, and to jump powerfully in athletics, basketball and netball.

> **Key term**
>
> **Power:** The ability to combine strength and speed.

▶ A high jumper generates power from their lower body to drive off the ground and over the bar. A golfer generates power using their upper body to create high club head speed, to hit the ball as far as possible off the tee.

## Testing power

There are two different, but similar, fitness tests for measuring power:

**1** Vertical jump test     **2** Standing long jump test.

### Vertical jump test

**Objective:** Jump as high as possible to demonstrate power in your lower body.

**Protocol:**

**1** Conduct a suitable warm up, if necessary.

**2** Stand side-on to a wall and reach up with the hand closest to the wall. Keeping your feet on the ground, mark or measure the point on the wall where the top of your fingertips touch. This is your standing reach.

**3** Put chalk on your fingertips. Stand away from the wall and jump vertically as high as possible, using both arms and legs to help you propel your body upwards. Touch the wall at the highest point of the jump.

**4** Measure the distance in centimetres (cm) between your standing reach and the highest point of the best of three jumps.

| | Male | Female |
|---|---|---|
| Excellent | > 65 cm | > 58 cm |
| Above average | 50–65 cm | 47–58 cm |
| Average | 40–49 cm | 36–46 cm |
| Below average | 30–39 cm | 26–35 cm |
| Poor | < 30 cm | < 26 cm |

◀ Normative data for 16–19-year-olds for the vertical jump test.

*Source: Davis, B. et al. Physical Education and the Study of Sport, 4th edn., Mosby Publishing, 2000.*

### Standing long jump test

**Objective:** Jump as far as possible to demonstrate power in your lower body.

**Protocol:**

**1** Conduct a suitable warm up, if necessary.

**2** Stand with your feet facing forwards and slightly apart, at the start of a safe landing area.

**3** Without a run up, and using your arms and legs to propel your body forwards, jump as far as you can. Be sure not to fall backwards on landing.

**4** Measure the distance in centimetres (cm) between your start point and the first point of contact on landing, usually the back of your heels. Record the best of three jumps.

| | Male | Female |
|---|---|---|
| Excellent | > 240 cm | > 190 cm |
| Above average | 217–240 cm | 173–190 cm |
| Average | 201–216 cm | 158–172 cm |
| Below average | 185–200 cm | 127–157 cm |
| Poor | < 185 cm | <127 cm |

◀ Normative data for 15–17-year-olds for the standing long jump test.

*Data: www.exrx.net/Testing/YouthNorms.html*

# 1.2.8 Flexibility

**Flexibility** is the range of movement available around a joint. The more flexible you are, the easier it is for you to move your body into sporting positions and the less likely you are to injure yourself.

▶ Flexibility is important in many sports. For example, good flexibility allows dancers and gymnasts to move their bodies into unusual positions. It also allows games players to execute dynamic movements.

> ### Key term
>
> **Flexibility:** The range of movement available around a joint.

## Testing flexibility: sit and reach test

**Objective:** Reach as far as possible to demonstrate flexibility at the hip.

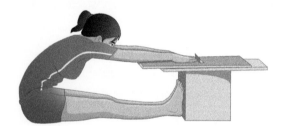

**Protocol:**

1  Conduct a suitable warm up, if necessary.

2  Sit on the floor with your legs straight out in front of you. You should have bare feet.

3  Put the soles of your feet, shoulder width apart, against the sit and reach box. Make sure your knees are flat against the floor.

4  Reach gently forwards, towards and beyond your feet, with your hands on top of each other and your palms facing down. Reach as far as possible, taking care to avoid bouncing.

5  After three practice reaches, hold the fourth reach for at least two seconds.

6  The distance in centimetres (cm) that your fingers touch on the sit and reach box is your score.

▼ Normative data for the sit and reach test.

|  | **Male** | **Female** |
|---|---|---|
| Super | > 27 cm | > 30 cm |
| Excellent | 17–27 cm | 21–30 cm |
| Good | 6–16 cm | 11–20 cm |
| Average | 0–5 cm | 1–10 cm |
| Fair | –8 to –1 cm | –7 to –0 cm |
| Poor | –20 to –9 cm | –15 to –8 cm |
| Very poor | <20 cm | <15 cm |

*Source: www.topendsports.com/testing/norms/sit-and-reach.html*

# 1.2.9 Agility

Agility is the ability to change direction at speed while maintaining control and balance. The best examples of agility are seen in sports where it is key to evade opposition players. Netball, rugby, basketball and boxing all provide opportunities to see performers being agile.

### Key term

Agility: The ability to change direction at speed; nimbleness.

▶ In rugby, changing direction at speed is important because players need to try and beat defenders while still moving forward.

## Testing agility: Illinois agility test

**Objective:** Run around the course as quickly as possible, trying not to slow down as you change direction through the cones.

**Protocol:**

1 Choose a non-slip surface and set up the course as shown in the diagram.

2 Conduct a suitable warm up, if necessary.

3 Lie down on your front with your head towards the starting line and your hands by your shoulders.

4 When the stopwatch is started, get up as quickly as possible and run around the course in the direction shown. The time taken to reach the finish line is recorded in seconds.

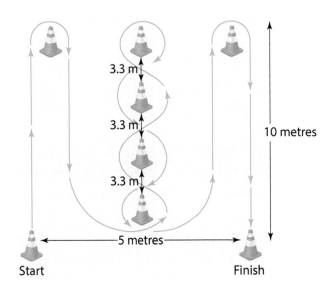

▼ Normative data for 16–19-year-olds for the Illinois agility test.

|  | Male | Female |
|---|---|---|
| Excellent | < 15.2 seconds | < 17.0 seconds |
| Above average | 16.1–15.2 seconds | 17.9–17.0 seconds |
| Average | 18.1–16.2 seconds | 21.7–18.0 seconds |
| Below average | 18.3–18.2 seconds | 23.0–21.8 seconds |
| Poor | > 18.3 seconds | > 23.0 seconds |

*Source: Davis, B. et al. Physical Education and the Study of Sport, 4th edn., Mosby Publishing, 2000.*

**Balance** is the ability to keep your body stable by maintaining your centre of mass above your base of support. In gymnastics, this is seen when performers hold shapes or execute dismounts. In games activities, balance is needed to stay upright when under pressure from opponents.

▶ The beam, where gymnastics skills are performed on a very narrow surface, provides the ultimate balance challenge in sport.

## Testing balance: stork stand test

**Objective:** Hold a stork balance for as long as possible.

**Protocol:**

1 Conduct a suitable warm up, if necessary.

2 Start by standing on both feet with your hands on hips.

3 Lift one foot and place it against the knee of your standing leg.

4 Raise the heel of the standing leg so that you are standing on tiptoes. A stopwatch should be started at this point.

5 Balance for as long as possible without letting either the heel of your standing foot touch the ground or the lifted foot move away from the knee.

6 At the point when the heel of the standing foot goes down or the raised leg leaves the standing knee, stop the stopwatch and record your result in seconds.

> **Key term**
>
> **Balance:** The ability to keep your body stable by maintaining your centre of mass above your base of support.

▼ Normative data for 16–19-year-olds for the stork stand test.

|  | **Male** | **Female** |
|---|---|---|
| Excellent | > 50 seconds | > 30 seconds |
| Above average | 41–50 seconds | 23–30 seconds |
| Average | 31–40 seconds | 16–22 seconds |
| Below average | 20–30 seconds | 10–15 seconds |
| Poor | < 20 seconds | < 10 seconds |

*Data: Johnson, B.L. and Nelson, J.K.* Practical Measurements for Evaluation in Physical Education, 4th edn., *Burgess, 1979.*

# 1.2.11 Co-ordination

**Co-ordination** is needed in all sports because it is the ability to move different body parts together effectively. Whether you are running, jumping, catching, hitting or throwing, you need to co-ordinate numerous body parts to perform successfully. Often people refer to hand–eye co-ordination in sport, but this is just one aspect of co-ordination.

▶ Co-ordination is particularly important for sports like cricket and tennis, where participants are required to co-ordinate their hands, feet, legs, arms, head and trunk.

## Testing co-ordination: wall throw test

**Objective:** Throw the ball against the wall, from hand to hand, as many times as possible in 30 seconds.

**Protocol:**

1. Mark a line on the floor two metres from the wall.

2. Conduct a suitable warm up, if necessary.

3. Stand behind the line and face the wall with a tennis ball in one hand.

4. When the stopwatch is started, throw the tennis ball against the wall with your left hand, using an underarm action, and catch it with your right hand.

5. Then throw the ball against the wall using your right hand, and catch it with your left hand.

6. Continue to throw and catch with alternate hands for 30 seconds, counting the number of completed catches.

> **Key term**
>
> **Co-ordination:** The ability to move different body parts together effectively.

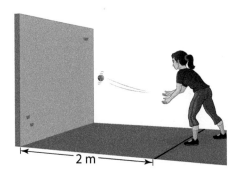

▼ Normative data for 14–16-year-olds for the wall throw test.

|  | Score (in 30 seconds) |
|---|---|
| Excellent | > 35 |
| Above average | 30–35 |
| Average | 25–29 |
| Below average | 20–24 |
| Poor | < 20 |

*Data: Beashel, P. and Taylor, J.* The World of Sport Examined, *Thomas Nelson and Sons, 1997.*

**Reaction time** is the time taken to respond to a stimulus. Examples of sporting stimuli include a starting pistol in athletics and a shot hit at a goalkeeper in hockey.

> ## Key term
>
> Reaction time: The time taken to respond to a stimulus.

▶ Sprinters need to have excellent reaction time in order to leave the blocks quickly after the starting pistol fires, while a hockey goalkeeper needs to react quickly to a shot coming in from close range.

## Testing reaction time: reaction time ruler test

**Objective:** React quickly to a ruler being dropped and catch it as soon as possible.

**Protocol:**

1   A partner holds a metre ruler between the outstretched index finger and thumb of your dominant hand.

2   The top of your thumb should be level with the 0 centimetre line on the ruler.

3   When you are ready, your partner should drop the ruler. You should catch it as soon as possible after it has been dropped.

4   Record the distance the ruler dropped, from the 0 centimetre line to the top of your thumb, in centimetres.

▼ Normative data for 14–19-year-olds for the reaction time ruler test.

|  | Score |
|---|---|
| Excellent | > 7.5 cm |
| Above average | 7.5–15.9 cm |
| Average | 15.9–20.4 cm |
| Below average | 20.4–28 cm |
| Poor | < 28 cm |

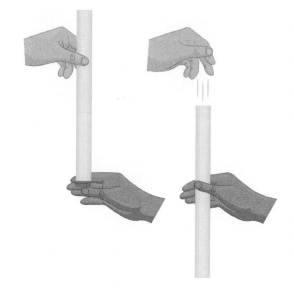

*Source: Davis, B. et al. Physical Education and the Study of Sport, 4th edn., Mosby Publishing, 2000.*

Regardless of their level of performance, everyone who commits time to training wants to see improvement. In order to make progress during a training programme, you must apply the **principles of training**. These principles ensure training is effective.

Effective training results in adaptations to your body. Adaptations are positive changes that bring improved performance. A programme that does not apply the principles of training will be less effective and may not result in improvements in performance. Successful athletes do not just train hard, they also train effectively; they apply the principles of training.

## Key term

**Principles of training:** Guidelines that, when applied, ensure that training is effective and results in positive adaptations. The principles of training are: specificity, overload, progression and reversibility.

## Study tip

The principles of training, effective training and positive adaptations link very closely with the information on the long-term effects of exercise on pages 40–45.

There are four principles of training:

**Specificity**

**Overload**

**Reversibility**

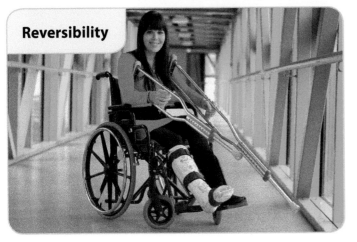

**Progression**

# The principles of training: specificity

In order for a training programme to be effective, it must be specifically designed with the performer and the sporting activity in mind. It must apply the principle of **specificity**.

To achieve appropriate adaptations, a sportsperson needs to train their body to be better at the things specially required by the activity they want to excel at. They must also consider their personal training requirements and design a training plan that improves their weaker areas. Training that applies the principle of specificity will, therefore, consider:

● the components of fitness most needed in the performer's activity

● the muscle groups required for the activity

● the aerobic or anaerobic nature of the activity (its intensity and duration)

● the strengths and weaknesses of the individual performer.

As a result, it should come as no surprise that swimmers will do a lot of their training in the pool and cyclists will do a lot of their training on a bike. It will also be no surprise that endurance swimmers will swim further in training than sprint swimmers, while sprint cyclists will train more powerfully than endurance cyclists.

## Key term

**Specificity:** Training must be matched to the needs of the sporting activity and the individual.

## Study tip

When considering specificity, review the following:

● The location of the major muscle groups on page 13.
● Aerobic and anaerobic exercise on pages 32–33.
● The components of fitness on pages 48–62.

## Activity

4   How would the following athletes apply the principle of specificity in their training? Think about the components of fitness they need to compete successfully, the key muscle groups they use and the aerobic/anaerobic nature of their activities? You may wish to do some research on the internet.

▲ Tirunesh Dibaba: 10,000 metre runner

▲ Jason Kenny: sprint cyclist

▲ Duncan Scott: 100 metre and 200 metre freestyle swimmer

# The principles of training: overload

A sportsperson's body will only adapt if it is forced to do so as a result of challenging training, if the sportsperson applies the principle of **overload** and pushes themself beyond their comfort zone. As the body recovers from the increased stress placed on it, positive adaptations take place.

If a performer trains at a level that is comfortable for them, they will not be applying the principle of overload and their body will not need to adapt. No training effects will be seen and their training will have been ineffective.

**Key term**

Overload: A greater than normal stress that is applied to the body, causing training adaptations to take place.

◀ It is important for people looking to make muscular gains to use weights that are challenging. While working at high intensity is likely to result in aches and pains in the short term, in the long term muscles will adapt and become stronger through the process of hypertrophy (the increase in size of skeletal or cardiac muscle).

◀ It is crucial for people looking for cardiovascular-respiratory gains to work at challenging intensities, where their heart rate is high. This will be uncomfortable at the time but, over a period of weeks, they will see positive adaptations and improved cardiovascular endurance.

# The principles of training: progression

The principle of **progression** is all about maintaining overload throughout a training programme. If a performer's training has been effective in the opening weeks of their programme, their body will have adapted and they will be more capable than they were when they started training. If they continue to train at the same level, then no further adaptations will take place, because the training will now be comfortable for them and they will no longer be applying the principle of overload.

In order to develop further, they need to make their training harder; they need to apply the principle of progression. This can be done by gradually increasing the frequency, intensity or time of their training, or by changing the type of training they are doing.

Examples of the principle of progression being applied include:

- Starting to train three times a week rather than twice a week.

- Running two miles rather than one mile in a single training run.

- Leg pressing 50 kg for eight reps rather than 45 kg for eight reps.

- Altering training from continuous training to interval training.

## Key term

**Progression:** Gradually increasing the frequency, intensity or time of exercise, or changing the type of exercise, in order for the body to continue to adapt through overload.

## Study tip

The elements of FITT, explained on page 68, can be used to apply the principle of progression and re-establish overload.

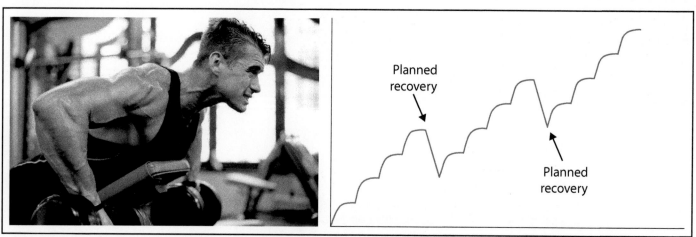

▲ By making sure there is gradual progression in a training programme, overload is maintained and the body continues to develop.

Training adaptations are only temporary. If training stops or reduces in intensity, the gains that have been achieved will be lost relatively quickly. Fitness development will, in essence, reverse. This is sometimes referred to as de-training.

Occasions when sportspeople will experience **reversibility** include:

- when they cannot train because of an injury

- when they do not train regularly enough

- when they do not train effectively

- during the off-season

- when they take a break from training for personal reasons

- when they prioritise other components of fitness. For example, speed may reduce if a performer focuses on cardiovascular endurance for an extended period of time.

Knowing about reversibility is important for two main reasons. First, knowing about it means you can make sure it does not happen as a result of poor motivation or poor planning. Second, if you are injured, knowing about it means you will recognise that you need to give yourself time following rehabilitation to build back to your previous levels of fitness, and that this time should be planned into your training programme. Returning to challenging training too soon after an injury is likely to slow recovery or cause you to re-injure yourself.

### Key term

**Reversibility:** Any adaptation that takes place as a result of training will be lost if you stop training.

### Activity

**5** Billy Vunipola of Saracens and England had to pull out of the 2017 British and Irish Lions summer tour to New Zealand because of a shoulder injury. As the Lions tour only every four years, and the competition to be selected is fierce, this must have been a difficult time for him.

**a)** What training advice would you have given to Billy to reduce the effects of reversibility during the summer of 2017 while his shoulder healed?

**b)** Following his shoulder treatment and rehabilitation, what would Billy have needed to consider as he prepared for the 2017/18 season?

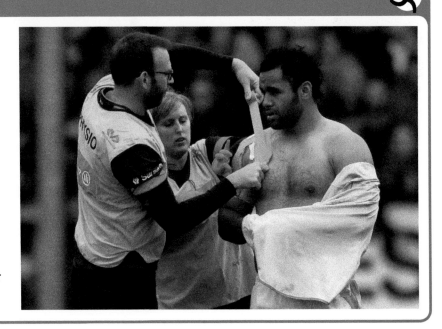

**FITT** is an acronym used to remind people of the four ways that training can be altered to achieve overload and progression.

Training programmes usually last six to eight weeks. Training must get harder through a training programme in order for a sportsperson to keep developing their components of fitness, and continue improving their sporting performance. FITT gives the four key variables that can be manipulated in training.

 **requency**

*The number of times training takes place*

- Increasing the number of training sessions in a given week achieves overload and progression.

- Because adaptation occurs during rest and recovery, it is important to incorporate suitable breaks between similar training sessions and not to over-train.

- Many people alternate the areas of their bodies that they train on different days to allow time for recovery.

 **ntensity**

*How hard the training is*

- Training harder achieves overload and progression.

- By working at a higher heart rate or by using heavier weights, cardiovascular endurance or strength/power/speed gains continue to be achieved.

- Raising the intensity of a training session may mean that the training time needs to be reduced.

 **ime**

*How long you train for*

- Training for longer achieves overload and progression.

- This could be going on longer runs, rides or swims. It could also be doing more repetitions in weight training. Using time to make training more challenging often assists a performer to develop their cardiovascular or muscular endurance.

**T ype**

*The method of training used*

- Changing the type of training used gives the body's systems a fresh challenge, thereby achieving overload and progression.

- This could be moving from continuous training to interval training or it could be introducing plyometric exercises into your weight-training programme.

There are a number of different types of training a performer can include in their training programme, including:

- continuous training
- fartlek training
- interval training.

Other methods of training are similar to interval training:

- HIIT (high intensity interval training)
- circuit training
- weight training
- plyometric training.

Before choosing a type of training, a performer should consider which components of fitness they should be focusing on. Strength and power athletes are likely to use a different mixture of training types from those used by endurance athletes. Strength and power athletes are likely to use a combination of interval training, weight training and plyometrics, while endurance athletes are more likely to use continuous training, fartlek training and interval training.

## Continuous training

**Continuous training** involves working at a steady intensity in the aerobic training zone for at least 20 minutes. Continuous training can involve running, cycling, swimming or rowing, providing that the activity is performed without rests or changes in intensity within the aerobic training zone.

> **Component of fitness trained:**
> Cardiovascular endurance
> Muscular endurance

When a performer is working at 60–80 per cent of their maximum heart rate (MHR) they are said to be working in the **aerobic training zone**. This means that they are working at a low enough intensity to allow oxygen to be delivered to the working muscles and used to release energy, but at a high enough intensity to achieve overload.

**Maximum heart rate** (MHR) is estimated as follows: 220 minus the age (in years) of the performer. This means a 15-year-old has a guide maximum heart rate of 205 beats per minute.

The aerobic training threshold marks the point at which overload is achieved. The performer's heart rate must be above this threshold, above 60 per cent of MHR, for the training to have an impact on their aerobic fitness. The anaerobic threshold, at 80 per cent of MHR, marks the point at which the performer begins to work anaerobically.

**Study tip**

Selecting the most appropriate type of training is one way of applying the principle of specificity.

Type of training is one element of FITT, and can be varied to achieve progression and overload.

**Key terms**

**Continuous training:** Training that involves working a steady intensity with no rest intervals. It can be performed at any intensity within the aerobic training zone.

**Aerobic training zone:** When a performer is working at 60–80 per cent of their maximum heart rate (MHR) they are working in the aerobic training zone. This means that they are working at a low enough intensity to allow oxygen to be used to release energy, but at a high enough intensity to achieve overload.

**Maximum heart rate:** The highest achievable heart rate for an individual.

◀ During continuous training, performers need to ensure that their heart rate is steady at a high enough level to achieve overload. It must be above the aerobic training threshold. Wearing a heart rate monitor during training enables performers to monitor their heart rate.

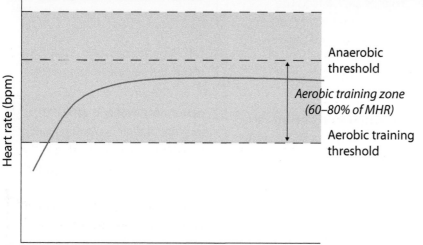

| Advantages of continuous training | Disadvantages of continuous training |
|---|---|
| • Doesn't require expensive equipment. | • Can be boring. |
| • Good for beginners because it is straightforward. | • Takes a long time. |
| • Can mimic aspects of endurance performance. | • Doesn't improve anaerobic fitness. |
| • Good to build aerobic endurance fitness during pre-season training or at the beginning of a training programme. | |

**Activity**

6   Estimate your guide maximum heart rate (MHR = 220 – age) and then calculate your aerobic training threshold and anaerobic threshold. What should your heart rate be to achieve aerobic overload?

# Fartlek training

Fartlek is a Swedish term meaning 'speed play'.

**Fartlek training** is a blend of continuous and interval training. While the exercise is ongoing, like in continuous training, the intensity rises and falls, like in interval training. The performer's heart rate moves from the aerobic training zone into the **anaerobic training zone** and back again.

When a performer is working at 80–90 per cent of their MHR they are working in the anaerobic zone. The high intensity means that the body is forced to produce energy without oxygen, which means lactic acid will accumulate. Improving the body's ability to delay, and then cope with, the accumulation of lactic acid is the main benefit of fartlek training, as it is with interval training.

Fartlek training is traditionally done outdoors over a variety of terrains. A training session might consist of a jog for three or four minutes, followed by a 40-second sprint, followed by a 40-second walk, followed by a further jog phase. Landmarks such as hills, trees or street signs can be used to trigger the next change of speed.

**Component of fitness trained:**
Cardiovascular endurance
Muscular endurance

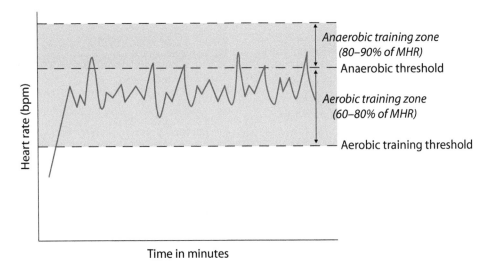

▼ During fartlek training, intensity – measured using heart rate – rises and falls. The bursts of high intensity push the performer into the anaerobic training zone which, over time, results in adaptations. It pushes the anaerobic threshold higher, allowing the performer to work aerobically at higher intensities.

| Advantages of fartlek training | Disadvantages of fartlek training |
|---|---|
| • More interesting than continuous training.<br>• Doesn't require expensive equipment.<br>• The periods of different intensity can be manipulated to allow for specificity.<br>• Training around the anaerobic threshold improves both aerobic and anaerobic fitness.<br>• Working around the anaerobic threshold has been shown to increase aerobic fitness very quickly.<br>• Improves the body's ability to delay, and then cope with, the accumulation of lactic acid.<br>• Good for activities where the intensity changes a lot, such as games activities. | • Some knowledge of the principles of training is needed to ensure intensity is managed correctly.<br>• High motivation is needed to enable the performer to increase the intensity when required. |

# Interval training

**Interval training** comprises pre-determined periods of work separated by pre-determined periods of rest. The rest periods allow a performer to work at a very high intensity during the periods of work.

**Component of fitness trained:**
Interval training can improve cardiovascular endurance and muscular endurance or speed and power depending on the relative length of the intervals.

Interval training can be modified to achieve the desired training outcomes. Relatively short intervals of work, separated by longer intervals of rest, develop anaerobic fitness, namely speed and power. Longer intervals of work, separated by shorter intervals of rest, develop aerobic fitness, namely cardiovascular endurance and muscular endurance. The number of times the work and rest intervals are repeated can also be altered depending on the performer's specific requirements and performance capabilities.

During the periods of work the performer is working in the anaerobic training zone, and during the periods of rest the performer's heart rate lowers into the aerobic zone, allowing some recovery before the next period of work. Over time, adaptations take place that result in the performer's anaerobic threshold rising. The performer's body will also become better at removing lactic acid and tolerating any lactic acid that accumulates. They will, therefore, be able to work aerobically at a higher intensity for longer.

## Activity

7  a)  Take part in a continuous training session, a fartlek training session and an interval training session. Monitor your heart rate regularly throughout all three sessions and draw three heart rate graphs to show the differences between the three types of training.

   b)  Compare and contrast the heart rate graphs.

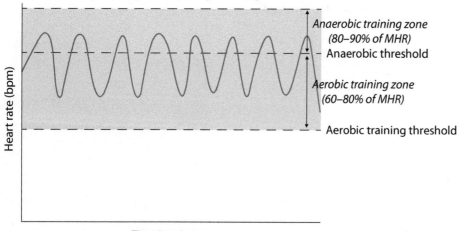

Anaerobic training zone (80–90% of MHR)
Anaerobic threshold
Aerobic training zone (60–80% of MHR)
Aerobic training threshold

*Heart rate (bpm)*

*Time in minutes*

◀ Interval training sees the intensity of work rise and fall in a uniform fashion. The rest periods allow higher intensity to be achieved during the work periods than in fartlek training. These very high intensity work periods have been shown to result in rapid adaptations quickly enhancing performance.

| Advantages of interval training | Disadvantages of interval training |
|---|---|
| • Training around the anaerobic threshold improves both aerobic and anaerobic fitness. <br><br> • Working around the anaerobic threshold has been shown to increase aerobic fitness very quickly. <br><br> • Improves the body's ability to delay, and then cope with, the accumulation of lactic acid. <br><br> • Doesn't require expensive equipment. <br><br> • Flexible and can be adjusted easily to suit the needs of the performer. <br><br> • Doesn't require long training sessions. | • Participants need to be motivated to tolerate the discomfort of the high intensity work periods. <br><br> • Longer recovery time between training sessions is needed than with less intense types of training. |

# High intensity interval training (HIIT)

**High intensity interval training (HIIT)** is, as its name suggests, a form of interval training that involves alternating between periods of very intense work in the anaerobic training zone and periods of active recovery in the aerobic training zone.

HIIT sessions often use traditional circuit training exercises, sometimes with added resistance, using weights or resistance bands, to ensure a full body workout in a very short period of time. This method is very popular with those looking for rapid fitness gains or rapid weight loss, as it is possible to burn a lot of calories in a short period of time.

**Component of fitness trained:**
HIIT can improve cardiovascular endurance and muscular endurance or speed and power depending on the relative length of the intervals.

## Key term

**High intensity interval training (HIIT):** Training that involves alternating between periods of very intense work in the anaerobic training zone and periods of active recovery in the aerobic training zone.

◄ HIIT sessions are generally relatively short, with participants working at very high intensity for short periods, with periods of active recovery when heart rate is not allowed to drop too low. The exercises used can be adjusted to meet the specific needs of those taking part but often include squats, lunges, burpees, mountain climbers and squat thrusts.

| Advantages of HIIT | Disadvantages of HIIT |
| --- | --- |
| • Doesn't require a lot of space. | • Participants need to be motivated to tolerate the discomfort of the high intensity work periods. |
| • Can be used to develop aerobic and anaerobic fitness. | |
| • Can be used for a whole body workout. | • Longer recovery time between training sessions is needed than with less intense types of training. |
| • Training sessions can be short. | |
| • Very flexible; sessions can be designed to meet the specific needs of the participants. | • Equipment is required for certain exercises. |
| • Rapid fitness development is possible. | |
| • Good for weight loss because many calories are burned in a session. | • Participants need to know how to perform the exercises safely so they do not injure themselves. |
| • Groups of people can train together. | |

## Activity

8   Find a video of a HIIT session on the internet and take part. Note the very high intensity of the workout by occasionally monitoring your heart rate.

# Circuit training

**Circuit training** generally involves six to ten different exercises, called stations, which are done one after the other in a series. The exercises can be laid out in a circuit, so participants move from one station to the next without the need to move equipment. Participants perform a set number of repetitions of each exercise at each station, or perform each exercise at each station for a set period of time, before moving on to the next exercise. Depending on the performer's level of fitness, they may choose to execute the circuit more than once in a session.

While the exercises in a circuit training session are very similar to the exercises in a HIIT training session, the circuit training focuses more on muscular development than cardiovascular fitness. That said, a well-designed circuit can give participants a whole body workout that develops a number of components of fitness.

Typical circuit training exercises include press-ups, sit-ups, burpees, squat thrusts, mountain climbers, triceps dips, squats, shuttle runs, lunges and skipping. When planning a full body circuit, it is often a good idea to alternate the body parts worked so that fatigue does not reduce the quality of movement technique.

**Component of fitness trained:**
Circuit training can improve all components of fitness depending on the exercises in the circuit and the way the circuit is organised.

## Key term

**Circuit training:** A series of exercises performed one after another at stations, which focus on different muscle groups.

◀ Circuit training requires participants to execute a number of repetitions of an exercise before moving on to the next one.

| Advantages of circuit training | Disadvantages of circuit training |
|---|---|
| • Doesn't require a lot of space. <br><br> • Can be used for a whole body workout. <br><br> • Very flexible; sessions can be designed to meet the specific needs of the participants. <br><br> • Groups of people can train together. | • Participants need to be motivated to tolerate the discomfort of the high intensity work periods. <br><br> • Longer recovery time between training sessions is needed than with less intense types of training. <br><br> • Equipment is required for certain exercises. |

## Activity

9  **a)** Design a circuit with six to eight stations/exercises to develop muscular endurance.

   **b)** Select another component of fitness and add two stations/exercises designed to develop that component.

## Weight training

**Weight training** involves the use of free weights and/or resistance machines to overload muscles and achieve adaptation.

Heavier weights can be used to achieve hypertrophy and an increase in strength, while lighter weights can be used to increase muscular endurance, which often brings a more toned physique.

- Strength goals: Lift 70 per cent of your 1 Repetition Maximum. Perform three sets of six reps, with three-minute rest intervals between each set.

- Muscular endurance goals: Lift 50 per cent of your 1 Repetition Maximum. Perform four sets of 12 reps, with two-minute rest intervals between each set.

◀ The bench press is a well-known weight training exercise that increases upper body strength, and the strength of the pectorals especially.

### Free weights

Free weights include dumb-bells, barbells and kettlebells.

Use of free weights develops muscles as fixators, as well as developing muscles as agonists and antagonists. This is because the performer has to stabilise their body and avoid unwanted movements while lifting the weights. Technique is, therefore, very important when using free weights, to ensure that the correct muscles are isolated and developed.

Lifting weights in a controlled way, with good technique, is also essential if you want to avoid injury. Working in pairs, with your partner acting as a 'spotter', is advisable; especially if you are working towards hypertrophy and strength goals because the weights will be heavier, increasing the risk of injury.

## Resistance machines

Resistance machines are excellent for those relatively new to weight training. Good technique is promoted because the movements are fixed by the design of the machine. However, while this reduces the chance of injury, it does also limit the development of fixator muscles.

Resistance machines found in most fitness centres include the pec fly, the chest press, the shoulder press, the leg press, the leg extension, the leg curl, the triceps extension, the low/long row and the lat pull down.

▼ The lat pull down machine is used to develop the latissimus dorsi muscles along with other upper body muscles.

| Advantages of weight training | Disadvantages of weight training |
| --- | --- |
| • Most effective type of training for developing strength. | • Requires equipment, which can be expensive to access. |
| • Can develop strength, power and muscular endurance, depending on the programme followed. | • More expertise is needed than for some other types of training. |
| • The programme can be very easily tailored to an individual's specific requirements. | • There is a risk of injury when lifting heavy weights. |
| • Lots of variety available, so it's more interesting than many other types of training. | • 'Spotter' required for certain exercises. |
| | • Appropriate rest between sessions is needed for muscles to recover and repair. |
| | • Muscle soreness is felt in the days following a training session. |

# Plyometrics

**Plyometrics** involves the use of high impact exercises to train muscles to contract more powerfully. A muscle is lengthened, often achieved through a landing, before being contracted, often achieved by leaving the ground again. It is the performer's ability to produce a strong contraction quickly that results in power, because power is the ability to combine strength and speed.

Sportspeople who need to perform powerful movements are likely to use plyometrics in their training programmes. Over time, they will develop the strength and speed of their muscular contractions, resulting in increased power.

▼ Plyometrics uses explosive movements, such as leaps, jumps and other movements where the body is pushed off the ground.

**Key term**

Plyometrics: Training that involves jumping, bounding and hopping exercises.

| Advantages of plyometrics | Disadvantages of plyometrics |
|---|---|
| • Very little equipment is needed. | • Appropriate rest between sessions is needed for muscles to recover and repair. |
| • Plyometric exercises mimic sporting actions. | • Good levels of strength are needed prior to taking part in a plyometric training session. |
| • Good at developing power, if training is done properly. | • High impact exercises can cause stress to joints. |
| | • Muscle soreness is felt in the days following a training session. |

**Activity**

10 Research, plan and carry out a plyometrics training session.
   a) Find three or four plyometric exercises and decide how many repetitions of each exercise you will include in your training session.
   b) Following your session, evaluate how regular plyometric sessions, like the one you've just done, could impact different aspects of your sporting performance.

# Warming up

A **warm up** prepares the body and mind for the physical activity to follow. Completing a warm up before taking part in physical activity is very important. Failing to warm up properly will reduce the quality of the performance that follows and also increase the chance of sustaining an injury.

There are five parts to an effective warm up:

## 1 Pulse raising

It is important for performers to raise their heart rate slowly before taking part in strenuous exercise by jogging or taking part in light cycling or rowing.

The benefits of this are: It increases blood flow and kick-starts the vascular shunt mechanism, increasing the volume of oxygen being delivered to the working muscles. It raises body temperature, which warms the muscles and prepares them for the activity ahead. Finally, it improves blood flow by reducing the viscosity of the blood. Warm blood flows more easily than cool blood.

> ▶ Jogging and low intensity skill practices can be used as pulse raisers at the start of a warm up.

> ### Key term
>
> **Warm up:** Preparatory exercises done to prepare the body and mind for physical activity.

## 2 Mobility

Preparing joints for activity, by moving them through their full range of movement in a controlled manner, is as important as preparing muscles. The benefits of this are: Ligaments and tendons are warmed and become more pliable. This increase in pliability reduces the risk of injury because it makes sprains and ruptures less likely.

◀ Exercises like shoulder circles, arm swings, side bends, leg swings, lunges and lateral rotations of the neck increase joint mobility prior to training or competition.

## 3 Stretching

The flexibility of muscles is temporarily improved by stretching during a warm up.

The benefits of this are: The speed and strength of muscle contractions are increased. Stretched muscles are less prone to strains and tears.

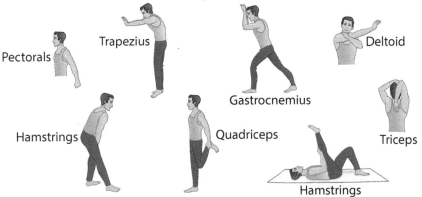

◄ Examples of some of the most common stretches.

## 4 Dynamic movements

Dynamic movements, such as high knees, heel flicks, side steps and high skips, mimic sporting actions and prepare the muscles and joints for the more explosive movements that are to come.

The benefits of this are: The pliability of muscles and the range of movement available at joints is further increased, increasing flexibility. Elevated cardiac and respiratory values are also maintained.

## 5 Skill rehearsal

The final part of the warm up takes performers very close to full intensity and provides them with an opportunity to practise the skills they will use during the full performance or the main part of the training session.

The benefits of this are: It helps performers ensure skills are performed to the best of their ability. It also gives a performer time to psychologically prepare and 'get into the zone', so they operate at their peak from the very beginning of the match, race or competition.

◄ Steph Curry has a very well established pre-match skill rehearsal routine, including ball-handling drills that involve two basketballs, lay-up shots and three-pointers.

### Activity

11 Plan and run a warm up for a small group. Take the group through each part of the warm up and explain why it is important as you do so.

# Cooling down

An effective **cool down** allows the body's systems to gradually recover after exercise. By continuing physical activity, but at lower intensity, waste products such as lactic acid can be removed more quickly. A cool down, therefore, helps to limit muscle soreness and stiffness in the days following exercise, which allows training to continue.

There are two parts to an effective cool down:

## 1 Low intensity exercise

A cool down is, in essence, the reverse of a warm up. It helps the body transition back to a resting state. As a result, the intensity of the activity needs to be low; allowing the performer to reduce tension and become more relaxed. Very slow jogging, swimming or cycling keeps limbs moving and helps to maintain blood flow to muscles.

The benefits of this are: The heart rate, breathing rate and body temperature drop gradually during the cool down. This maintains the circulation of an increased volume of blood and oxygen for some time after training or competing. This, in turn, encourages the body to continue to remove lactic acid, stopping it from pooling in the muscles. If lactic acid is not removed from the body it can cause discomfort in the hours after exercise.

## 2 Stretching

Stretching is then carried out, with the major muscles used in the activity held in a stretched position for longer than they were in the warm up.

The benefits of this are: It reduces muscle soreness and stiffness in the days following a training session, and aids recovery.

▶ The cool down should reduce in intensity and stretches should be held for longer than they were during the warm up.

**Key term**

Cool down: Less strenuous exercises, following on from more intense activity, where physiological activity is allowed to gradually return to normal resting levels.

**Study tip**

The key word when discussing cool downs is 'gradual'. A cool down allows the heart rate, breathing rate and body temperature to drop *gradually*.

**Study tip**

If you feel dizzy, nauseous or overly stiff after exercise, it could be an indication that your cool down was not executed properly.

**Activity**

12 Plan and run a cool down for a small group. Take the group through each part of the cool down and explain why it is important as you do so.

Injuries in sport are inevitable. While some activities bring higher risks than others, taking part in any sport or physical activity comes with a chance of injury. That said, it is the responsibility of coaches, teachers, lawmakers, officials and the participants themselves to do all they can to reduce the risks.

▶ Concussion has received a lot of press recently and rugby union has responded to concerns from the medical community with new tackle laws, new head injury assessment (HIA) protocols and new return-to-play procedures.

## Minimising the risk of injury

There are a number of different ways to minimise the risk of injury.

### Personal protective equipment

Many sports have personal protective equipment to protect against the most likely injuries. While some equipment is mandatory and must be worn, some is merely optional. Helmets in equestrian and cycling are mandatory, while gumshields in rugby and helmets in cricket remain optional for adult participants.

▶ When defending penalty corners, hockey players can put masks on to protect themselves.

### Activity

**13** Play 'personal protective equipment ping pong' with a partner. One of you names an item of personal protective equipment used in a sport, then the other one does the same. Keep going until one of you fails to think of something. The last person to name an item wins.

## Correct clothing and footwear

The requirements of certain sports make specific types of clothing more appropriate. Lycra in athletics and cycling, shorts for many games activities and jodhpurs and jackets for those involved in equestrian, are some of the more obvious examples. Before sports participation, performers should also remove jewellery and ensure that their clothing doesn't have fastenings that could cause injury to themselves or to other participants. Participants who might experience bad weather, such as kayakers, rock climbers and skiers, should all dress appropriately for the conditions, and be prepared for the weather to change unexpectedly.

Sport-specific footwear is available for almost all activities. Studs and spikes are worn for outdoor sports like football, golf, rugby, athletics and cricket, where slipping could be an issue. Soft-soled shoes with high levels of grip are worn for indoor activities like badminton, netball, volleyball, table tennis and squash. Protection is also offered in sports like cricket, where batsmen have reinforced toes in their boots.

▶ Basketball boots have ankle support, which helps to absorb impact and adds stability. In a sport where performers jump very high and then land, the design helps avoid ankle and knee injuries.

## Appropriate level of competition

The rules and regulations of most sports prevent young performers playing outside of their age category. In contact and combat sports like rugby league, rugby union and boxing, these rules are especially important to ensure that young people are not placed in high-risk situations. For example, in many contact sports, boys and girls are only permitted to train and compete in mixed groups until around the age of puberty, when some boys grow quickly and develop a more muscular build than girls of the same age.

◀ By having age categories in sports, national governing bodies try to ensure that the level of competition is appropriate for the participants.

## Lifting and carrying equipment safely

Sports like gymnastics, trampolining, athletics and table tennis use heavy equipment that needs to be moved into place before the activity can begin. In fitness centres, people also need to take care when moving heavy weights or benches.

Here are some guidelines on how to lift and carry equipment safely.

- Ensure those lifting and carrying are physically capable and know how to lift and carry safely.

- Discuss the lifting and carrying process with the other people involved before you begin, so that everyone knows what will happen, and continue to communicate effectively throughout the movement.

- Before moving an item, ensure that the area where the item will be placed is clear and the route to that area is free from obstructions.

- Ensure you have enough people helping, to make the lifting process as easy as possible.

- Never bend at the waist to lift and lower an object. Always bend from the knees; lift by straightening your legs and lower by bending your legs, keeping a straight back all the time.

- Ensure fingers do not get trapped underneath an object when putting the equipment down.

## Use of warm up and cool down

Failing to warm up properly means that muscles, joints and connective tissues are unprepared for the physical challenges of participation, making injuries more likely. There should always be enough time allowed for a full warm up, with all five parts of the warm up executed properly.

Following exercise, a cool down helps the body recover and ensures that participants do not feel unduly stiff and sore in the hours and days following exercise.

### Study tip

The benefits of warming up and cooling down are discussed in detail on pages 78–80.

### Activity

**14** Write a short report evaluating how certain rules in one of your chosen physical activities protect participants from injury.

Different sporting settings are likely to contain different hazards and, therefore, present different risks. While at elite level numerous people will be employed to prepare playing areas and ensure that risks are kept to a minimum, at youth and community level everybody must take responsibility for identifying hazards and reducing risk.

## Potential hazards in sports halls

- Open doors
- Equipment left lying around
- Damaged equipment
- Damaged floor
- Water/sweat on the floor making it slippery
- Short run-off areas, because courts are close to the walls

## Potential hazards in fitness centres

- Open doors and windows
- Weights and equipment left lying around
- Damaged equipment
- Water/sweat on the floor making it slippery
- Other people involved in activities like skipping
- Participants with a poor understanding of their fitness levels or health problems

## Potential hazards on playing fields

- Nearby buildings or fencing
- Trees, bushes, stinging nettles and brambles
- Litter
- Animal excrement
- Goal posts that could be run into
- Poor pitch surface

## Potential hazards on artificial outdoor areas

- Fencing
- Litter
- Animal excrement
- Goal posts or empty post sockets
- Poor pitch surface
- Wet and slippery surface

## Potential hazards in swimming pools

- Large body of water
- Cleaning products and pool chemicals
- Wet and slippery surface
- Equipment left lying around
- Lane ropes lying by the side of pool
- Sharp floor surfaces, which will cause problems for people with bare feet
- Unconfident swimmers

## Activity

15  a)  Walk around your school and conduct a risk assessment for each of the areas that you observe. Look for potential hazards and assess the risk of each hazard as low, moderate or high.
    b)  Suggest ways that the level of risk for each hazard can be reduced.

## What should be done to minimise risk?

- Check for potential issues regularly.
- Put away all equipment when you have finished using it.
- Clean equipment and floors regularly.
- Fix or replace damaged items.
- Supervise participants in high risk areas, such as swimming pools and fitness centres.
- Provide induction sessions for participants so they know how to use equipment safely with the correct techniques.
- Ensure participants are fit and healthy enough to take part in activities.

# Practice questions

1  Which **one** of the following is a test for strength?
   Put a tick (✓) in the box next to the correct answer.
   A  Vertical jump test  *powe*  ☐
   B  30-metre sprint test  *speed*  ☐
   C  Illinois agility test  *agility*  ☐
   D  1 Repetition Maximum test  ☑
   **[1]**

2  Which **one** of the following is **not** an item of
   personal protective equipment?
   Put a tick (✓) in the box next to the correct answer.
   A  Equestrian helmet  ☐
   B  Football boots  ☑
   C  Boxing gumshield  ☐
   D  Cricket batting gloves  ☐
   **[1]**

3  Which **one** of the following is the best example of
   the specificity principle of training?
   Put a tick (✓) in the box next to the correct answer.
   *progression*
   A  A marathon runner who runs for extended
      periods during training.  ☑
   *frequency*
   B  A shot-putter who makes their training
      harder every three weeks.  ☐
   C  A rugby player who trains regularly to
      avoid losing fitness.  ☐
   D  A netball player who works outside their
      comfort zone during training.  ☐
      *overload*
   **[1]**

4  Which **one** of the following statements is false?
   Put a tick (✓) in the box next to the correct answer.
   A  Agility is the ability to change direction
      at speed.  ☐
   B  Power is the combination of strength
      and speed.  ☐
   C  Reaction time is the time taken to respond
      to a stimulus.  ☐
   D  Co-ordination is maintaining your centre
      of mass over your base of support.  ☑
   **[1]**

5  Using practical examples, explain the importance
   of cardiovascular endurance in sport.  **[4]**

6  A warm up is seen as important before
   sporting activity.
   Describe **three** components of an effective
   warm up.  **[3]**

7  Outline what is meant by plyometric training.  **[2]**

8  Define the following principles of training:
   A  Overload
   B  Progression
   C  Reversibility  **[3]**

9  Describe two types of training suitable for an
   endurance athlete.
   Compare the two types of training.  **[6]**

10 Different sport settings present different hazards
   to participants.
   Describe the potential hazards in two different
   sporting settings. Discuss which setting you
   consider most hazardous.  **[6]**

When you have worked through this chapter, you will have developed knowledge and understanding of:

- physical activity and sport in the UK
- participation in physical activity and sport
- the commercialisation of sport
- ethics in sport
- drugs in sport
- violence in sport.

# I love playing. I just love winning slightly more.

There are many physical, emotional and social benefits of participating in physical activity. Understanding trends in participation across different social groups in the UK allows providers of sports and physical activities to target groups with low participation rates. If the barriers that make it more difficult for these target groups to take part are identified and removed, then participation will increase and more people will experience the physical, emotional and social benefits of taking part in sport and physical activity.

UK Sport, Sport England and the national governing bodies of each sport all collect data that helps identify trends in participation rates of different social groups in different physical activities and sports on behalf of the Department of Digital, Culture, Media and Sport. This data is then used to determine how funding is distributed to increase participation.

### Trends in participation across different social groups

In the UK, it is generally understood that:

- younger people are more physically active than older people

- men are more likely to be physically active than women

- people from ethnic minority backgrounds are less likely to be physically active than people from white British backgrounds

- people with disabilities are less likely to be physically active than people without a disability

- people with higher-paid jobs are more likely to be physically active than people with lower-paid jobs.

However, in recent years there has been a rising trend in women and people with a disability participating in sport and physical activity. This follows efforts to target funding and promotional campaigns at these social groups to encourage them to get active.

**Study tip**

The physical, emotional and social benefits of participating in sport and physical activity are discussed in detail on pages 135–38.

▼ These graphs, from Sport England's 2015–2016 Active Lives survey, demonstrate trends in participation among different social groups in the UK.

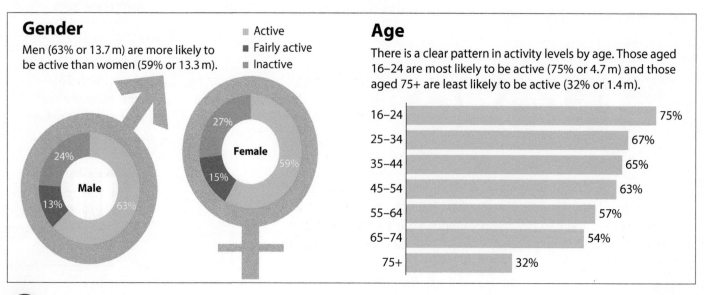

**Gender**

Men (63% or 13.7 m) are more likely to be active than women (59% or 13.3 m).

- Active
- Fairly active
- Inactive

Male: 24%, 13%, 63%

Female: 27%, 15%, 59%

**Age**

There is a clear pattern in activity levels by age. Those aged 16–24 are most likely to be active (75% or 4.7 m) and those aged 75+ are least likely to be active (32% or 1.4 m).

| Age | |
|---|---|
| 16–24 | 75% |
| 25–34 | 67% |
| 35–44 | 65% |
| 45–54 | 63% |
| 55–64 | 57% |
| 65–74 | 54% |
| 75+ | 32% |

## Trends in participation across different physical activities and sports

Sport England's Active Lives survey collects data about the different types of sport and physical activity that people in the UK aged over 16 are involved in. Looking at the trends, we can see that many people are involved in walking. Although walking is recognised as a physical activity, which will have health and fitness benefits, it is not normally reported with sporting and fitness activities data.

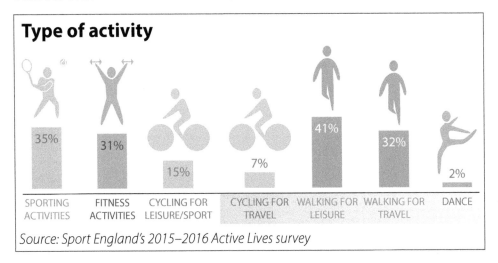

**Type of activity**

| SPORTING ACTIVITIES | FITNESS ACTIVITIES | CYCLING FOR LEISURE/SPORT | CYCLING FOR TRAVEL | WALKING FOR LEISURE | WALKING FOR TRAVEL | DANCE |
| --- | --- | --- | --- | --- | --- | --- |
| 35% | 31% | 15% | 7% | 41% | 32% | 2% |

*Source: Sport England's 2015–2016 Active Lives survey*

If we look more closely at the sporting activities that people are involved in, we can see that swimming, athletics, cycling, football and golf are the most popular sports.

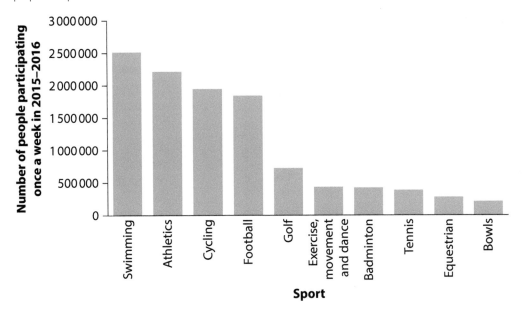

When you analyse and evaluate the trends, it is clear to see that many more people are involved in physical activity for leisure, travel and fitness reasons than are involved in organised and competitive sport. This is important information to have when deciding how to increase the general activity levels of the nation.

**Activity** DATA

1 Choose a sport and research participation rates in the UK, using data from the sport's national governing body. For example, the Football Association (FA) collects data about football and England Netball collects data about netball.

2 Find out what the Department of Digital, Culture, Media and Sport (DCMS) is and what it does.

**DATA**

## Collecting and analysing data about trends in participation

Sport England's Active Lives survey is carried out regularly. It collects **quantitative data** and **qualitative data** about participation among different social groups in the UK.

Quantitative data is usually collected using closed questions. These are questions that have a defined answer. An example of a closed question is:

How often do you exercise?

☐ More than three times a week

☐ Three times a week

☐ Twice a week

☐ Once a week

☐ Less than once a week

If you ask enough people closed questions, you will have data that you can present in a table or as a pie graph, line graph or bar graph.

Qualitative data is usually collected using open questions. These are unstructured questions that gather a wide range of information about how the person completing the questionnaire feels, thinks and behaves. Examples of open questions include:

- How do you feel about sport and exercise?

- Describe anything that would prevent you doing more sport and exercise.

- What would need to be in place for you to participate in sport and exercise more often?

It is much harder to present, interpret and analyse qualitative data. Often researchers read completed questionnaires carefully and tease out trends. A trend is information that is being repeated by a significant proportion of the people who completed the questionnaire and that can be used to describe the general direction in which something is developing at any given moment.

Analysing trends in qualitative data allows you to make predictions about what people who didn't complete your questionnaire might think or feel about the issues you are investigating.

### Key terms

**Quantitative data:** Data that measures things and involves numbers. Quantitative data gives you an objective answer to your question.

**Qualitative data:** Data that focuses on gaining a deeper understanding of people's thoughts and opinions. Qualitative data gives you a subjective answer to your question.

### Activity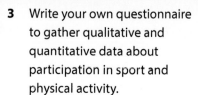

3   Write your own questionnaire to gather qualitative and quantitative data about participation in sport and physical activity.

a)   You want to find out what kinds of physical activity people do, how often they do it, and what encourages or discourages them from taking part, so use a mixture of open and closed questions.

b)   Ask people from different social groups to complete your questionnaire.

c)   Analyse and evaluate the responses. What do they tell you about participation in sport and physical activity where you live? Does your data fall in line with national trends?

Quantitative and qualitative data collected from and about social groups that do not participate in physical activity and sport has helped develop an understanding of the many different factors that affect participation.

**Factors affecting participation in physical activity and sport**

Age    Gender    Ethnicity    Religion/culture    Disability

Role models    Family

Media coverage    Environment/climate

Opportunity/access    Education

Cost/disposable income    Time/work commitments    Discrimination

The factors affecting participation overlap. An individual will often experience more than one of them at the same time, and will experience a different combination of factors at different times in their lives. For example, people with disabilities may suffer from discrimination, have limited role models and issues with opportunity and access.

**Activity**

4  **a)**  Use this spider diagram to create a mind map, linking related factors together. For example, 'discrimination' can link to age, gender, religion/culture, ethnicity and disability.

   **b)**  Looking at your mind map, can you see reasons why certain social groups have lower than average participation levels?

While there are many different factors that affect participation in physical activity and sport, there are five major factors that have been shown to have a huge influence on a person's activity levels.

## Age

Participation tends to peak between the ages of 16 and 25, after which it slowly drops away. This is why it is crucial to engage young people in school sport, because it has been shown that those who are fully involved at a young age are more likely to stay active as they get older.

As people get older, their general fitness decreases and this can impact on their level of participation. Bone strength, muscular strength, flexibility, stroke volume and tidal volume all decrease. This means older people are more likely to suffer injuries, will take longer to recover from injuries and are more likely to have health issues that prevent them from participating. However, staying active into old age can slow this process of physical deterioration, which means people who stay active tend to live longer than people who live a sedentary lifestyle.

As people get older they also take on more social responsibilities. As they have children and are promoted to more demanding jobs, for example, they have less free time and less disposable income. Finding the time and the money for sport and exercise, therefore, becomes less of a priority for people in the middle of their lives. It is only when people retire that they begin, again, to have the time to participate.

There is also a feeling in society that sport and exercise are the pastimes of the young. This can lead to **discrimination** against older people. This perception is reinforced by professional sportspeople retiring in their mid-thirties, limiting the number of older role models.

### Activity

5   Research the range of sports and physical activities that are on offer at your local leisure centre. Does the centre cater for all age groups? Are there any age groups that are under-represented or over-represented? Can you suggest reasons why?

◀ Many of the older people who are keen to stay active will change the sports that they are involved in. When games like netball, football and hockey become too physically challenging, sports like bowls and golf provide opportunities for people to continue to participate, with a much lower risk of injury.

# Gender

More boys and men are involved in physical activity and sport in the UK than girls and women. This is due to many different reasons, including discrimination against women. For example, until 1972 women were not permitted to run distances over 800 m because the distances were considered too strenuous for them. Female recreational runners, as well as elite female runners, now run marathons every weekend across the world, which highlights just how poorly informed such thinking was.

However, although discriminatory attitudes towards women in sport are slowly changing, there still remains an imbalance in media coverage, financial support and, consequently, spectator numbers. This is heightened by the fact that many national governing bodies and media companies are run by men, as are many of the companies that sponsor sportspeople; men who promote men's sport over women's sport. The knock-on effect is that there are fewer opportunities for women to compete at a professional level, fewer girls aspire to be professional sportspeople and, as a result, fewer visible female **role models**. Fewer girls see sport as a priority in their lives. Not only do girls and women experience fewer opportunities than boys and men to participate once they have left school, but they are also less likely to access the opportunities that are open to them.

Yet, in recent years, change has begun to gather pace. Recent successes by UK women in rugby, football, cricket, gymnastics, athletics and hockey have gained good media coverage and there has been an increase in the number of girls and women taking part in these sports as a result. In addition, national campaigns, such as Sport England's 'This Girl Can' campaign, are tackling the out-dated idea that exercise is unladylike and should, therefore, be avoided, which is seen as essential to motivating more girls and women to participate.

◀ GB won hockey gold at the Rio 2016 Olympics, creating a real buzz around hockey and women's sport.

# Ethnicity, religion and culture

The term '**ethnicity**' describes the ethnic group you belong to. An ethnic group is a social group that shares cultural traditions, a religion, a language or other factors. The term '**culture**' describes the ideas, customs and social behaviour of a particular social group.

As a multicultural society, it could be assumed that participation in physical activity and sport in the UK would be the same across all ethnic groups. This is not always the case.

Data shows that participation by people from ethnic minority backgrounds is often limited to sports traditionally associated with that ethnic group. This is probably because people from ethnic minority backgrounds lack role models they can identify with in other sports. Also, while it would appear that ethnic minority groups are well represented in some professional sports, this doesn't always translate to participation at grass-roots levels. Furthermore, the number of professional captains, coaches and managers from ethnic minority backgrounds remains low in most popular sports, fuelling debate about the level of racial discrimination in professional sport.

Cultural and religious traditions can also have an impact on participation in sport and physical activity. For example, some religions have periods of time when people fast, days when food intake is very limited, and it is more difficult to be physically active when your energy levels are low. Some cultures also have dress codes that make participation more challenging, and cultural differences in the role of women in society can explain why women participate in sport and physical activity less in some cultures.

## Key terms

**Ethnicity:** Describes the ethnic group you belong to. An ethnic group is a social group that shares cultural traditions, a religion, a language or other factors.

**Culture:** The ideas, customs and social behaviour of a particular social group

▲ Cricket remains very popular among young people from Caribbean, Indian and Pakistani backgrounds because of the long-standing tradition of playing the game and the numerous role models in these countries.

## Study tip

Remember that ethnicity and culture are not interchangeable terms. There can be more than one cultural tradition within an ethnic group.

## Activity  DATA

**7** Write some questions about this graph for your partner to answer.

▶ This graph shows participation by ethnic group for 16 to 25-year-olds in 2014.

Graph: participation by ethnic group.

**Male** — White-British, White-Other, Asian, Black, Chinese, Mixed, Other

**Female** — White-British, White-Other, Asian, Black, Chinese, Mixed, Other

Scale: 0%, 20%, 40%, 60%

*Source: www.sportengland.org*

▼ In some cultures, dress codes prevent athletes from competing in the usual sport-specific attire.

# Disability

Disability is defined by the government as a physical or mental impairment that has a substantial and long-term effect on a person's ability to carry out normal daily activities. It can, therefore, affect a person's participation in sport and physical activity. However, national governing bodies make efforts to ensure their sports are accessible to all, and participation rates among people with disabilities are on the increase.

## Activity | DATA

**8** **a)** Analyse this graph. What does it tell you?

    **b)** Discuss the reasons for this positive trend.

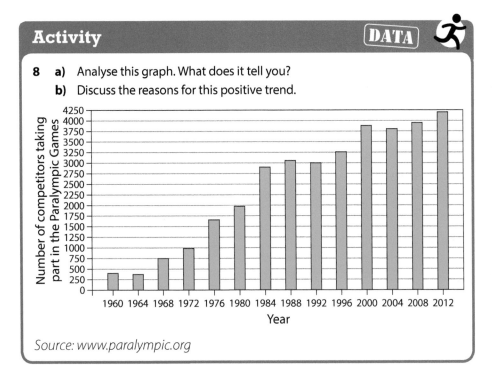

*Source: www.paralympic.org*

▲ In 2004, at the age of nine, swimmer Ellie Simmonds decided that she was going to the Paralympics. She is now a five-time Paralympic champion and has numerous world records to her name.

An increase in media coverage of sport involving participants with disabilities has resulted in a corresponding increase in the visibility of role models like Ellie Simmonds, which increases the sporting aspirations of young people with disabilities in the UK.

However, despite the fact that participation rates are on the increase, people with a disability are less likely to participate in sport and physical activity than people without a disability. This is because there are still significant barriers in place that make participation more difficult for people with disabilities. There are a limited number of teachers and coaches with the necessary qualifications to facilitate sport for people with disabilities, as well as a lack of appropriate facilities.

▶ Wheelchair versions of sports have adapted rules and different tactics, so having specialist coaches is essential if they are going to be engaged in effectively.

# Upbringing

Your friends and family, where you grow up and where you go to school, are all factors that affect participation in sport and physical activity.

## Family

If an individual's family is positive about sport and exercise, then it is more likely that they will be too. By providing transport, money and equipment, a supportive family makes it much easier to participate. By aspiring to follow in a family member's footsteps, a young person with sporting role models in their family is also far more likely to participate.

The reverse is also true. If a person's family does not have a history of taking part in sport and are not hugely supportive, then it is far less likely that they will participate.

Families with little disposable income can find it hard to afford the costs associated with membership, equipment and transport even if they do encourage participation. That said, some sports are relatively inexpensive and schools and communities often work hard to provide young people from lower income families with opportunities to participate.

▶ The Redknapps are just one example of a child following a parent into professional sport. Similar examples are extremely common in amateur-level sport. Mothers and daughters playing for the same rugby club for example.

## Education

The place someone goes to school is likely to play a big part in whether or not they actively participate in sport and physical activity. It is also likely to impact on the type and range of sporting opportunities they are given. While some schools invest heavily in PE and sport provision, other schools need to, or choose to, allocate their funds differently. The number of PE staff and coaches and the quality of sports facilities often determine the role sports play in the everyday life of a school.

In addition, some schools are less effective in educating their students about the benefits of a healthy active lifestyle. Students in these schools are less likely to understand the importance of participating in sport and physical activity as part of a healthly active lifestyle, which will have an impact on their interest in participation throughout their lives.

▶ Private schools in the UK are very well known for having excellent facilities and coaches. They are also able to offer sporting scholarships to talented students. It is little wonder that many professional sportspeople have come through the private school system.

**Study tip**

It is a trend that people in lower-paid jobs participate less in sport and physical activity than people with higher-paid jobs, and a person's upbringing tends to have an impact on what type of job a person does in adult life.

**Activity**

9  Research the sports facilities and opportunities for participation in sport and physical activity at a private school and at a state school near you. What differences do you notice?

## Friends

A person's friendship group will have an extremely big impact on their level of participation in sport and physical activity. While most people choose friends that have similar interests to them, friends can have a powerful influence over the choices a person makes. 'Peer pressure' can be a positive force, promoting participation in sport, but it can also be a negative force if a friendship group actively discourages participation.

▶ Groups of friends can often be found playing recreational sport together but there are lots of friendship groups that choose less active hobbies.

## Environment and climate

The place someone lives plays a huge part in how likely they are to participate in sport and physical activity. While some areas are blessed with excellent local sporting facilities and a wide array of clubs for people to join, other parts of the country are not so lucky.

For example, people living in urban, built-up areas, are less likely to have access to playing fields, making participation in grass-based sports like football and rugby more difficult. Similarly, the number and quality of swimming pools, courts, sports halls and fitness centres has an impact on the opportunities a person has to participate locally.

Finally, the climate can make certain sporting activities more or less accessible. Sports like cricket are more suited to places where the weather is warmer and sunnier. And snow-based sports, like skiing and snowboarding, are more popular in Scotland, where it usually snows in the winter, or close to indoor snow centres and dry slopes.

◀ Sporting facilities in urban areas are often in very high demand, which can limit access to physical activity for people living in the area.

Increasing promotion, increasing provision and increasing access are three strategies designed to improve participation.

## Promotion

Promotion is very important in increasing participation in sport and physical activity. Advertising the importance of leading an active, healthy lifestyle can help a person push it higher up their list of priorities. The media also plays a huge role in turning positive sporting role models into household names, giving people, especially young people, an example to follow.

▲ The heavily publicised success of British cycling, both track and road, alongside the obvious health benefits of the sport, has seen a huge surge in participation in cycling across the UK.

It is critical that sport and physical activity is promoted to everyone, but especially to the social groups that participate least. It is also crucial that lower-profile sports are given national coverage. Major sports – including football, rugby, tennis and cricket – have huge numbers of fans, large advertising budgets and often dominate newspaper and television reporting. Only by fully promoting the full array of sporting opportunities in the UK, including the opportunities associated with lesser-known sports such as squash, canoeing and lacrosse, will a wider group of people be encouraged to participate.

## Provision

It is challenging to take part in sport and physical activity if suitable facilities do not exist. Participation in some sports is also challenging without access to coaching sessions or a club to play for. Increased sporting provision – increasing suitable facilities, coaching sessions and clubs – for under-represented social groups and under-represented sports is critical, if overall participation in the UK is going to increase.

Increasing provision costs money. While large sums of money are generated by the National Lottery, and this funding is distributed by UK Sport, Sport England and other organisations, the current economic climate makes it difficult to find additional public money to spend on increasing provision. This situation is magnified by the fact that private companies prefer to offer their financial

**Study tip**

The relationship between sport, sponsorship and the media, which is called 'the golden triangle', is described on page 101.

◀ The National Lottery is a key source of income for sport in the UK. Funding is used to develop facilities and to support elite performers.

support to sports that are already popular and have a large media presence. Sponsoring these sports provides the best possible return on their investment. Smaller sports and less-popular physical activities, which may be enjoyed by hard-to-reach social groups, are not as attractive to sponsors, limiting the amount of funding available to them.

## Access

Access to facilities and coaching for a wide range of sports and for a wide range of people is clearly essential, if participation is going to be increased.

Sports facilities often need to make a profit and, as a result, tend to focus on sports and physical activities that bring in large numbers of people. For example, sports halls often run lots of indoor football sessions at the expense of alternatives like badminton, basketball and volleyball. While this does bring money into the facility and is great for people who enjoy playing football, it does little to increase participation in less popular activities. Facilities need to be encouraged to timetable a much broader range of activities to increase participation.

Another key to increasing participation is to ensure that everyone can access sessions without fear of discrimination or worries about cost. For example, facilities should be adjusted so they can be used comfortably and easily by people with disabilities, subsidised memberships should be offered to people with low incomes, and women who prefer not to exercise alongside men should have the option to attend 'women only' sessions. Together, steps like these will extend opportunities to participate to a wider group of people and bring those in hard to reach social groups into the sporting community.

▶ Increasing access can come in the form of additional sessions, improved transport links or equipment that allows groups of people to engage more easily.

**Activity**

10 How accessible are your school's sports facilities for someone who uses a wheelchair?
   **a)** Carry out an audit of your school's sports facilities, assessing how many of the activities on offer could be accessed by someone using a wheelchair.
   **b)** What needs to happen to improve the situation?

### Activity

**11** Read the case studies about Chloe and Jonathan.

**a)** Describe the relationship Chloe and Jonathan have with sport.

**b)** Which of the factors that affect participation, discussed on pages 91–97, apply to Chloe and to Jonathan?

**c)** Describe how Chloe has benefitted from participating in sport.

**d)** Jonathan has asked you for advice about how he could increase his physical activity. What would you advise him to do?

### Chloe

Chloe has a fairly active lifestyle. She works full time and has a young son, but she and her husband do their best to squeeze exercise into their busy lives.

Chloe started enjoying sport at school, where she was in the netball squad. She was also involved in local gymnastics and dance clubs. The PE department at her school offered her the opportunity to participate in a lot of different activities. The town where she grew up had good sports facilities, which often let children take part in activities for free. Her mum was always happy to drive her to and from practices and fixtures. She often gave a lift to her best friend, who did a lot of the same things as Chloe.

After school, Chloe went to university, where she joined the netball squad to meet people and make friends. She socialised with the squad after practice and was happy that she could keep fit while having fun.

Since leaving university and getting a job, Chloe still plays netball on a Saturday and trains with her team on a Tuesday evening. She lives quite near her parents, and they are happy to babysit when required. Playing netball helps her to unwind and stay in shape, and she enjoys socialising with her teammates.

### Jonathan

Jonathan is not very interested in sport and his working day is very long so he finds it difficult to set aside time for exercise. He joined a gym a couple of years ago, to try and lose some weight, but it was quite expensive and he did not go regularly enough to make it good value for money, so he did not renew his membership after the first year.

Jonathan did not consider himself sporty at school. He was quite keen to try out a few different sports at one point, but his friends encouraged him to play computer games with them. He had an opportunity to join a local cricket team one summer, as they were advertising for new players, but his mum and dad were too busy to drive him across town and the membership fees were not cheap. He was also a little worried that he would not fit in because he did not know anyone else, so he decided to give it a miss.

Jonathan lives alone with his cat, Tabs. He is really into films and spends most evenings in front of the television. He writes a film blog, something he really enjoys doing. He does not go out and socialise with friends all that often because, although he has a couple of good friends who live fairly close by, they both have children and struggle to find the time to see him. Jonathan is worried that he is unfit and a couple of minor health scares have increased his concerns.

# The commercialisation of physical activity and sport

**Commercialisation** is the management or exploitation of a person, organisation or activity in a way designed to make a profit.

Sport and physical activity is now big business, with companies connected with the sport and leisure industry making vast profits. The media and sponsors have played a big part in this commercialisation of sport and physical activity.

## The golden triangle

The **golden triangle** is a graphic representation of the interdependent relationships that exist between sport, the media and sponsorship. It is golden because of the huge sums of money involved. And it is a triangle because all three groups need to work together effectively to realise their collective potential; they are dependent on each other for success. Issues can arise if one of the groups forgets the importance of the other two and tries to dominate.

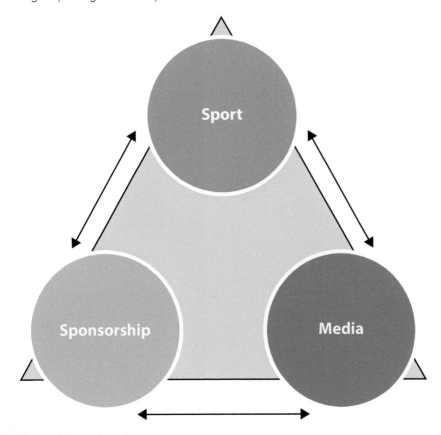

▲ The golden triangle

### Activity

**12** Discuss the golden triangle diagram. What benefits does each group get from working with the other two?

### Study tip

If you get a question on commercialisation in your exam, it may be worth sketching the golden triangle to help you plan your answer.

# The media and the commercialisation of physical activity and sport

The term 'the **media**' covers a diverse range of technologies that act as a means of mass communication with the public.

The media plays a central role in commercialising physical activity and sport. Television companies, in particular, pay huge sums of money for the rights to broadcast sporting events. And the more exposure the media gives to a particular sport or sporting event, the greater the potential for businesses to earn money from it. For example, an advert on a billboard at an English Premier League game will be visible to people watching the match all around the world. This will raise the profile of the product or service being advertised, and increase sales for the company that owns it.

**THE MEDIA**

## Key term

**Media:** A diverse range of technologies that act as a means of mass communication. The media informs, educates and entertains. The media consists of the print media (sometimes referred to as 'the press'), the broadcast media, the internet and social media.

### Broadcast media (television and radio)

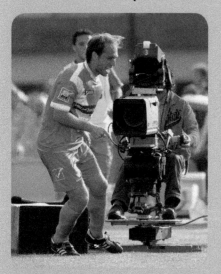 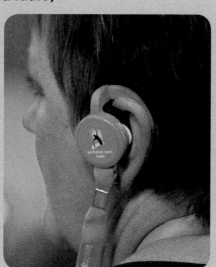

Companies pay to advertise on free-to-air television and people pay subscription fees to watch digital sports channels and pay-per-view matches or events. Digital radios allow people to listen to sporting action and discussion live while on the move, and digital radio stations can sell advertising.

## Activity

**13** How many different ways is sport featured on free-to-air television over the course of one day? Use a television guide to help you.

## Social media

Social media gives instant updates on what is happening in the world of sport. It also provides direct access to sports performers, some of whom have become celebrities because of this exposure. The more visible you are as a celebrity, the more you are able to earn in appearance fees and from sponsors. Social media has helped sports stars become more famous and so earn more money.

## The internet

The internet, accessed through computers, tablets and mobile phones, provides access to broadcast and print media. It also allows people to look at club websites, and sports-related merchandise and sporting equipment online.

## Print media (newspapers and magazines)

Daily and weekend newspapers have dedicated sports sections. There is also a huge array of sports magazines carrying interviews, insights and opinion on sporting matters. Both newspapers and magazines make money by selling advertising, as well as from the cover price.

# Sponsorship and the commercialisation of sport and physical activity

A **sponsor** is an individual or group, usually a company, which provides financial or other forms of support to an event, activity, person or organisation in return for some kind of commercial return. As a result of linking itself to a sportsperson, a sports team, a sporting event or a sports facility, a sponsor benefits from the successes associated with whatever they have sponsored. Sporting successes reflect positively on their brand. Their brand is also exposed to everyone who sees whatever they have sponsored. **Sponsorship** can take a number of different forms.

## Key terms

**Sponsor:** An individual or group, usually a company, which provides financial or other forms of support to an event, activity, person or organisation.

**Sponsorship:** The giving of money or goods to performers in order to get good publicity and/or increase profit.

### Financial support

Many sportspeople have personal sponsors who assist them financially with the day-to-day costs of living, training and competing. In return, the sponsor's name is linked to the performer and the performer is likely to mention them in interviews.

**SPONSORSHIP**

### Clothing, equipment and footwear

Sportswear and equipment brands will pay sportspeople to wear their shoes and clothing or use their brand of equipment. Companies will also pay sportspeople and sports teams to have their logos on their kit and equipment.

## Facilities

Many stadia are now named after brands as sports teams sell the naming rights for a large sum of money. Training grounds and other facilities can also be funded by sponsorship from large global companies.

## Study tip

It is important not to confuse sponsorship with advertising. Many companies can pay to advertise their products or services at a sporting event, but there are usually only a few sponsors. A sponsor has a much closer relationship with the event, activity, person or organisation that it is sponsoring.

It is also important not to confuse sponsorship with endorsements. When a sports performer is sponsored, they are given money, clothing, equipment or footwear to help them perform. When a sports performer endorses a product or a service, they are paid by a company to lend their image to advertising the product or service, which may not even be sport related.

## Activity

**14** Watch a sporting event on the television. List all the different sponsors you can spot. How easy is it to tell the difference between advertisers and sponsors?

# The positive and negative effects of the media and sponsorship

The media and sponsorship have both positive and negative effects on sport and physical activity.

| The positive effects of the media on sport and physical activity | The negative effects of the media on sport and physical activity |
|---|---|
| ✓ Takes sports to huge audiences. | ✗ Increases the pressure on participants to perform at their best all the time, which may reduce their enjoyment. |
| ✓ Coverage helps to increase interest in sport generally. | ✗ Media scrutiny means that mistakes on and off the field are broadcast far and wide. |
| ✓ Helps increase grassroots participation. | ✗ Gives coverage to poor behaviour by some sportspeople who are not good role models. This can have an impact on young people's behaviour. |
| ✓ Builds up the tension before an event, providing spectators with something to look forward to and get excited about. | ✗ Creates a gap between the sports regularly covered by the media and sports that receive less media coverage. For example, a gender gap exists because men's sports receive more coverage than women's sports. |
| ✓ Being in the media spotlight helps turn sportspeople into role models. | ✗ The media can influence opinion by choosing to emphasise one story or perspective over another. |
| ✓ Brings money into sport, which helps pay for facilities, coaching and technology for professional and grassroots sport. | ✗ Rules and timings of sports are altered to fit in with media requirements. |
| ✓ Brings sponsors who, in turn, bring more money into sport. | ✗ Supporters are required to pay large sums to watch sports. |
| ✓ Brings more money for wages for players in popular team sports, providing an incentive to people, particularly people from poorer backgrounds, to work hard towards their sporting goals. | ✗ More competition places huge physical demands on participants. |
| | ✗ Participants have to fulfil media obligations, like interviews, which can be a distraction. |
| | ✗ Participants can be overpaid which creates a divided society. |

| The positive effects of sponsorship on sport and physical activity | The negative effects of sponsorship on sport and physical activity |
|---|---|
| ✓ Brings money into sport, which helps pay for facilities, coaching and technology for professional and grassroots sport. | ✗ Can shift the focus from sport to business and money. |
| ✓ Allows individuals participating in sports that receive less money from other sources to go professional. | ✗ Increases the pressure on participants to perform at their best all the time, in order to retain their sponsorship, which may reduce their enjoyment. |
| ✓ Allows events to be run without costs being passed on to teams or participants. | ✗ Sponsors may expect a say in how a sport, a tournament, a club or a performer's life is run. |
| | ✗ Successful teams and individuals are more attractive to sponsors, which widens the gulf between the best and the second best. The good teams and individuals get better, while the poorer, second-best teams and individuals continue to struggle. |
| | ✗ Participants can be overpaid which creates a divided society. |

## Activity

15 Identify specific examples of the positive and negative effects of the media and sponsorship on sport and physical activity.

16 Hold a debate about whether commercialisation is good for sport.

   a) Divide into two equal groups and flip a coin to determine who debates for 'YES' and who debates for 'NO'.

   b) Spend some time in your groups thinking about the evidence that justifies your position.

   c) Ask your teacher to chair the debate.

## Study tip

When discussing advantages and disadvantages of commercialisation, it is important to use specific examples to illustrate each advantage and disadvantage rather than make sweeping statements.

If something is ethical, it is in accordance with accepted principles of right and wrong. Unethical conduct can give sports performers an advantage, but it usually reflects badly on them and their sport.

## Sportsmanship

**Sportsmanship** is conforming to the rules, spirit and etiquette of a sport. A huge part of sportsmanship is being gracious in victory and defeat, while respecting members of the opposition and officials. Examples of sportsmanship are examples of ethical behaviour, and the value of sportsmanship lies in the positive spirit of the game that it creates. Sportsmanship has huge value because it allows people to demonstrate that you can be competitive and driven while maintaining high personal standards and treating others with respect. This is clearly important in all aspects of life.

### Key terms

**Sportsmanship:** Ethical, appropriate, polite behaviour while participating in sport; fair play.

**Gamesmanship:** Where the laws of the game are interpreted in ways, which, while not illegal, are not in the spirit of the game; pushing the limits to gain an unfair advantage.

◀ Rugby is a sport where elements of sportsmanship are demonstrated regularly, despite its aggressive nature. Shaking hands at the end of a game in a calm and sporting manner, regardless of the result, is one demonstration of sportsmanship. Cricket is another sport where sportsmanship is very evident. Batsmen are clapped to the wicket and congratulated by fielders when they reach one hundred runs.

## Gamesmanship

**Gamesmanship** is attempting to gain an advantage by stretching the rules to the limit. This kind of behaviour often takes advantage of loopholes in the rules of a game and comes as a result of people placing a very high value on victory, sometimes at the expense of sportsmanship. There is frequent debate about where the line between gamesmanship and deviance should be drawn, whether gamesmanship is ethical or unethical. Examples of gamesmanship include time-wasting or designing tactics around a grey area in the rules.

▶ In basketball, players have worked out that deliberately fouling poor free-throw shooters could give them an advantage. Knowing that the player would be likely to miss their foul shots, the fouling team could then get the ball back without conceding points. In many sports, players employ tactics to delay and frustrate the opposition and to control the game clock to their advantage, and these are all examples of gamesmanship.

# Deviance

**Deviance** is unethical behaviour that goes against the spirit or rules of a sport. It happens when people lose control or are unable to maintain high personal standards, and does not reflect well on a person's character. It ranges from overt cheating and drug taking to arguing with officials or opposition players, fighting or behaving in any manner that is not appropriate in a sports environment.

Professional players are role models and, therefore, have an obligation to behave properly. So why does deviant behaviour occur? Most examples of deviant behaviour occur when a performer places winning above the need to behave ethically. Winning brings fame and potential fortune and, for some, this means they need to win, whatever the cost. It is also the case that some performers place less importance on playing by the rules and doing things correctly than others do. Performers, just like the rest of us, are a mixture of people who do all they can to do things correctly and stay on the right side of the law and people who do not.

▲ Intimidating officials: failing to respect referees in football has been a major discussion point in recent years, with the Football Association looking to stop this kind of deviance. Other notable examples of deviance in sport include reckless challenges, use of bad language, illegal betting on games and overt cheating by, for example, using performance-enhancing drugs.

## Key term

**Deviance:** Behaviour that is either unethical, immoral or seriously breaks the rules and norms of a sport.

## Study tip

It is important not to confuse sportsmanship, gamesmanship and deviant behaviour. You will need to be able to describe each of them accurately and provide appropriate practical examples of each of them.

## Activity

17 Come up with as many examples of sportsmanship, gamesmanship and deviance as you can.

# 2.1.11 Violence in sport

Unfortunately, **violence** is occasionally seen in sport. Contact sports are more likely to provide examples of violence, because they require players to be aggressive, which takes them closer to the point at which they lose control.

While a powerful rugby tackle or a hard challenge in football may be aggressive, providing the aggression is channelled towards sporting performance, it is not classed as violence. Violence is generally a sign that someone has lost control. Once a sportsperson injures or threatens to injure another performer, outside the rules of the game, with no sporting benefit, then they have behaved violently.

Violence in sport is most likely to occur when a performer:

- feels physically threatened, the 'fight or flight' response kicks in and they fight instinctively

- feels that additional aggression will be beneficial to their performance

- feels frustrated because they have performed badly or their team has performed badly

- feels angry because they believe they have been wronged by another performer or an official's decision

- is concerned that it may look weak to step away first.

Clearly, violence is a real concern in elite sport. The watching public, especially young people who idolise performers, may view the violent behaviour of their role models as acceptable and copy it. Obviously violence is not acceptable in sport or in wider society, and violent performers are removed from the sporting arena and given lengthy bans and large fines.

# Drugs in sport

Performance-enhancing drugs are substances that affect a performer's body and give them an unfair advantage over their competitors. They are banned, and it is every sportsperson's responsibility to ensure that they do not, knowingly or mistakenly, take a banned substance.

Some sportspeople have tested positive for a banned substance because they forgot to check what was in the medicine prescribed to them by their doctor. Some medicines contain banned substances, and it is up to athletes to carefully check their prescriptions.

## Why do sports performers use drugs?

The commercialisation of sport means that sporting success brings money, fame and high social status. The rewards of victory are so great that some performers will try anything, and risk everything, to win.

Training hard and training smart will improve performance, but many performers will never achieve top success legally. Perhaps they do not have the biological advantages of their competitors or perhaps they lack the inner drive required to train hard enough. Or perhaps they are being pressured by a teammate or a coach, who is telling them that everyone else is already doing it and they need to do it too in order to compete. Regardless of the reasons, they view performance-enhancing drugs as a quick way to improve their performance and achieve the success they crave.

## Performance-enhancing drugs and their effect on performance

### Anabolic steroids

Anabolic steroids are synthetic hormones that mimic the effects of the hormone testosterone. They:

- increase bone strength
- increase muscle growth
- increase strength, speed and power
- reduce training recovery time.

Performers involved in sports that require speed, power and strength would gain advantage from using anabolic steroids.

▶ Sprinter Dwayne Chambers served a drug ban for steroid use.

**Study tip**

It is often useful to produce lists of factors to revise from. For example:

The main reasons why performers use performance-enhancing drugs are:

1 Desire to achieve fame and fortune.
2 Fear that they cannot win naturally.
3 Pressure from others to be the best.
4 A win-at-all-costs attitude.
5 Knowledge that performance-enhancing drugs will improve their performance quickly.

## Beta blockers

Beta blockers reduce the effects of adrenaline, which is released by the body to speed up body systems in times of stress. Beta blockers:

- reduce heart rate
- reduce muscle tension
- reduce blood pressure
- improve fine motor control and precision.

Performers involved in sports that require them to execute movements calmly and under control, such as archery, shooting and diving, would gain advantage from using beta blockers.

▲ Pistol shooter Kim Jong-Su from North Korea tested positive for beta blockers in 2008.

## Stimulants

Stimulants affect the central nervous system, increasing arousal. They have been shown to:

- increase alertness
- increase energy
- reduce fatigue
- suppress appetite.

Performers competing in high-energy sports requiring lots of training would gain advantage from using stimulants.

▶ Sprinter Asafa Powell served an 18-month ban for using a banned stimulant.

# The impact of drug use in sport

The use of performance-enhancing drugs has significant negative impacts on the performers who take them and on sport more generally.

## The impact of drug use on performers

All drugs have negative side effects, so there are significant physical risks associated with taking performance-enhancing drugs, for example:

- anabolic steroids can cause depression and an increased risk of cancer, organ failure, high blood pressure, and infertility

- beta blockers can cause nausea, tiredness and heart problems

- stimulants can cause headaches, high blood pressure and anxiety and an increased risk of strokes.

Sports performers who take performance-enhancing drugs also experience psychological and social impacts. They are constantly worried about being caught and they will receive lengthy – sometimes life-time – bans from sport, will be stripped of their titles and sponsorship deals, and will receive worldwide condemnation if they are caught. Sports fans want a clean sporting world, and respect for much-loved performers disappears overnight when they are found to have been taking drugs. Even when they have served their bans, performers who have been caught cheating in the past can never win again without fellow performers and fans questioning whether they are training and competing fairly.

▲ A distraught Marion Jones admits to taking performance-enhancing drugs in 2007. She has been stripped of five Olympic medals.

## The impact of drug use on sport itself

When the results of races, games and competitions are not trusted completely, sport loses its integrity. It becomes tainted. Sports fans want to see fair competitions, where the most talented, hardest working and most capable, win. They do not want to see cheats beating people who have followed the rules. When clean athletes, who are not taking drugs, have to prove that they are clean and answer questions about whether they are cheating to win, sport loses something. It loses its magic.

### Activity

**19 a)** Identify three more examples of drug taking in sport.

   **b)** Look at the work of the World Anti-Doping Agency (WADA). What is its role in protecting the world of sport from drug cheats?

# Practice questions

1 Which **one** of the following is **not** an example of a type of media?
Put a tick (✔) in the box next to the correct answer.
A Television ☐
B Internet ☐
C Newspapers ☐
D Sponsors ☐
**[1]**

2 Which **one** of the following is **not** a trend describing participation in physical activity and sport?
Put a tick (✔) in the box next to the correct answer.
A Women are generally less physically active than men. ☐
B Disabled people cannot play sport. ☐
C Those from ethnic minority backgrounds participate less. ☐
D People with better-paid jobs participate more. ☐
**[1]**

3 Which **one** of the following is the best example of sportsmanship?
Put a tick (✔) in the box next to the correct answer.
A Not kicking the ball into the crowd when a decision goes against you. ☐
B Shaking hands and saying 'well played' at the end of a match. ☐
C Not arguing with an official. ☐
D Stopping a teammate being violent towards a linesman. ☐
**[1]**

4 Which **one** of the following statements is **false**?
Put a tick (✔) in the box next to the correct answer.
A A person's family will be a factor affecting their participation in sport. ☐
B The cost of an activity may prevent certain people from taking part. ☐
C Most people get into sports when they are young. ☐
D People with full-time jobs do not have time for sport. ☐
**[1]**

5 Describe how taking anabolic steroids will affect a performer. **[3]**

6 **Figure 1** shows participation rates in four sports between May 2012 and August 2012.

▲ **Figure 1**

Using **Figure 1**, identify the sport with the greatest increase in participation between May and June. **[1]**

7 Explain **two** strategies that can be used to improve sporting participation. **[2]**

8 Give three factors that could affect a person's participation in physical activity. **[3]**

9 The commercialisation of sport can be illustrated by the golden triangle.
Explain the golden triangle.
Discuss the positive and negative influences of commercialisation on sport. **[6]**

10 Ethics in sport links to the spirit of the game and the way that players conduct themselves.
Describe sportsmanship, gamesmanship and deviance.
Discuss which of these is most important in professional sport. **[6]**

# 2.2 Sports psychology

When you have worked through this chapter, you will have developed knowledge and understanding of:

- characteristics of skilful movement
- classification of skills
- goal setting
- mental preparation
- types of guidance
- types of feedback.

# The characteristics of skilful movement

**Motor skills** are learned body movements or actions that are created when muscles contract and cause movements at joints. High-level sporting performance relies on motor skills being performed **skilfully**. The main difference between most elite performers and most amateur performers is how skilfully the elite performer executes their motor skills and the consistency with which they do so.

## There are five characteristics of skilful movement:

1 Efficiency

2 Pre-determined

3 Co-ordinated

4 Fluent

5 Aesthetic

**1** Efficiency means there is little wasted effort or energy. The skill is made to look easy.

**2** Pre-determined means the result is intended. The performer knows exactly what they want to do, and they do it.

**3** Co-ordinated means that the performer uses different body parts together effectively.

**4** Fluent means that the movement is smooth and flowing.

**5** Aesthetic means that the movement looks good; that it is pleasing to the eye.

### Study tip

While one skilful movement is likely to show all the five characteristics of a skilful movement, it is better to use different examples to demonstrate characteristics separately.

### Key terms

**Motor skill:** A learned body movement or action that is created when muscles contract and cause movements at joints.

**Skilful movement:** A pre-determined, fluent and co-ordinated movement, which is efficient, technically accurate and aesthetically pleasing.

### Activity

1 Write a description of each of the characteristics of skilful movement. Include an example. You can use the photographs on this page to help you, or come up with your own examples. Be sure to describe what it is about the example that exemplifies the characteristic you are describing.

All sports and physical activities can be broken down into a group of motor skills that can be practised. For example, the motor skills involved in netball include passing, dodging, marking and shooting.

▲ Here we see Joanne Harten performing the netball-specific motor skills of shooting and passing.

A number of classifications are used to analyse and describe motor skills. They group different motor skills together based on shared characteristics, which is valuable when considering how they should be taught and coached for the most effective outcomes.

The classifications that you need to be aware of are:

- Difficulty (Simple ←——→ Complex)
- Environmental (Open ←——→ Closed)

Very few skills are, for example, completely closed or completely open. The extremes of each classification are, therefore, placed on a continuum, and skills are placed on the continuum between the extremes. The closer the skills are placed to an extreme, the more like that extreme they are.

Extreme A ←————————————→ Extreme B

### Study tip

The plural of continuum is continua. You need to know about two **skills continua**. However, each one is a continuum.

### Key term

**Skills continua:** A method of categorising skills along a continuum that acknowledges that, while all the skills placed on the continuum are different, they can all be grouped together according to their level of difficulty or the level of environmental influence.

### Study tip

To understand how continua work, imagine a continuum with 'Very tall' at one end and 'Very short' at the other end. You would know exactly where to stand if your class was placed on the continuum.

# Difficulty continuum (Simple ⟷ Complex)

The difficulty continuum considers how complicated skills are and how much focus and concentration are required to complete them:

- **Simple skills** have few **sub-routines** and require a relatively low level of focus to complete them. There is not a lot of information to process and/or few decisions to be made.

- **Complex skills** are the opposite. They are made up of lots of sub-routines and require great focus because they are very difficult. There is a lot of information to process and/or numerous decisions to be made.

## Key terms

**Simple skill:** A skill that consists of basic movements that are not difficult to perform and require few decisions to be made. For example, a chest pass or a straight up and down jump.

**Sub-routine:** Part of a motor skill. Together, the sub-routines of a skill make up the skill.

**Complex skill:** A skill that requires a lot of focus and decision-making to perform. For example, a twisting somersault.

▲ **SIMPLE**

Running 400 metres is a relatively simple motor skill because it has few sub-routines and a low level of focus is required to execute it. The race is more about tactics and athleticism than skill.

**COMPLEX** ▲

The twisting somersault in gymnastics is a complex motor skill. It has many sub-routines and high levels of focus are needed to perform it.

# Environmental continuum (Open ⟷ Closed)

The environmental continuum considers the factors that surround a performer as they execute the motor skill:

- **Open skills** are heavily affected by an unpredictable and changeable environment. The execution of the skill is influenced by conditions of play, teammates and opponents.

- **Closed skills** are the opposite. They are not affected by the environment because they are predictable. The timing of the skill is largely down to the individual involved and there are very few variables that are outside their control.

▲ **OPEN**

A rugby tackle is a very open motor skill that should be placed near the 'Open' extreme of the environmental continuum. The timing and style of the tackle is heavily influenced by many factors including the ball carrier, the tackler's teammates and the position on the pitch.

**CLOSED** ▲

A javelin throw is a very closed motor skill that should be placed near the 'Closed' extreme of the environmental continuum. The exact timing of the throw is down to the athlete, who is throwing the same weight javelin in a very similar environment each time.

## Activity

2 Get into small groups. Place two cones on the floor, about 10 metres apart. For each classification, label one of the cones with one of the extremes from the continuum. Each person should choose a different sporting skill and take it in turns to stand on the continuum where you think your skill should be placed. Explain your thinking as you go.

## Study tip

The exact placement of a motor skill on a continuum is debatable. It is important to apply the criteria when making a judgement but remember that this is not an exact science, so it is a good idea to pick obvious examples that are close to the extremes.

## Key terms

**Open skill:** A skill that is affected by the environment and must be adapted to suit the environment. These skills are usually externally paced. For example, a pass within a football game.

**Closed skill:** A skill that is performed in a predictable environment. For example, a player throwing into a line-out in rugby.

**Goal setting** is very important in sport and exercise as it links closely with motivation. Effective goal setting allows performers to improve and optimise their performance by giving training purpose and focus. Setting and working towards goals increases the chances of a person improving and being increasingly successful over time.

Effective goal setting can:

- motivate performers
- improve focus
- increase effort
- optimise performance
- develop perseverance
- improve performance
- increase adherence (commitment) to exercise and training programmes.

### Key term

**Goal setting:** The process of setting targets that a performer will work towards achieving.

### Study tip

Think of your target grades at school. Why do you have them? How do they make you think and feel when you get results back? Would you think and feel differently without them? If you think about why you have target grades in school and what they do, you'll be able to give a great answer to the question, 'Why is goal setting important in sport and exercise?'

### Activity

3   On the start line of any marathon, there will be lots of people with completely different goals from each other. Provided that the goals are appropriate for each individual, there is a chance that many will finish the race feeling successful, even though just one person was able to win the race.

a)   Discuss how lots of participants in a marathon can finish the race with a sense of success, even though they did not win the race.

b)   Describe three different goals that a marathon runner might have.

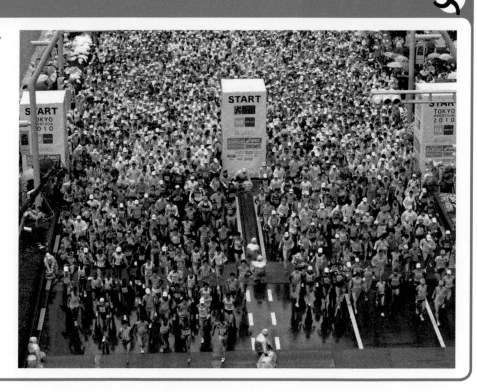

The way that goals are set is crucial. Setting goals that are too general and bordering on unattainable will only serve to demotivate performers; the exact opposite of what is wanted. Effective goals should be set by applying the **SMART** principle of goal setting.

## Key term

**SMART:** An acronym used to guide the setting of effective goals. SMART goals are specific, measurable, achievable, recorded and timed.

## Study tip

Collecting quantitative data on a regular basis can help you measure whether or not you are on track to achieve your goals.

### Achievable

Goals should be within the reach of the performer. They should be challenging but attainable. This is valuable because a performer will become demotivated if they don't achieve a goal. They are also unlikely to chase a goal they do not think is achievable. *For example, a striker setting a goal to score two more goals than last season.*

### Recorded

Goals should be written down, so that they are not forgotten, and cannot be easily altered when things get difficult. Recording goals sets them in stone and makes them more meaningful. *For example, goals can be written at the top of a training programme, to remind the performer about what they are trying to achieve.*

### Measurable

You must have a way of knowing if you have achieved your goals. Goals should, therefore, contain a time or something similar. This is valuable because it allows a definite 'met' or 'not met' statement to be made. *For example, a freestyle swimmer setting a goal to take 0.1 seconds off their 100 metre time.*

### Timed

Goals should have time limits. If they don't, a performer will always be working towards a goal, with no real rush to get there and no given point when they will be able to decide if they have been successful. This is valuable because a performer can assess whether or not they have hit their goal at any given point. *For example, a young athlete setting themselves the goal of running a 1500 metre race in under five minutes by the end of the following season.*

### Specific

Goals should target a specific aspect of performance to develop, which it is possible to actively focus on. This is valuable because it ensures that the goal emphasises a definite training need. *For example, a sprinter setting a goal around improving her drive phase.*

## The use of data in goal setting

Data on sporting performance is a useful tool when setting SMART goals. Collecting data on times in sprinting, distances in athletic throwing events, percentages of successful passes completed in games activities, percentages of successful serves in tennis or percentages of balls bowled on certain lengths in cricket, means challenging specific, measurable and achievable goals can be set.

Here are some examples of SMART goals:

- A 100 metre sprinter: Take 0.2 seconds off my personal best time by the last race of the season.

- Striker in football: Score 12 goals this season, compared to nine goals last season.

- Rugby goal kicker: To improve my season's kicking percentage by 5 per cent compared to last season.

- Trampolinist: To raise my difficulty tariff by 0.5 by the end of next month.

- Marathon runner: To take two minutes off my personal best in the marathon at the end of the month.

### Activity

4 Consider an area of your life where you would like to see some improvement. What is your goal? It could relate to sport and exercise or to your life more generally. Write down some SMART goals to help you achieve better in this area and then explain how your goals are SMART.

## Reviewing goals

It is not enough to set goals and work towards them. You must review them and decide whether or not success has been achieved:

- If the goals have been met, then new goals should be set to ensure continued motivation, and to push the individual to improve further.

- If the goals have not been met, then the process of evaluating why this was the case can often be extremely beneficial, and inform future training, and future goal setting.

▲ If a large goal, like winning the Rugby World Cup, has been set, then smaller goals will need to be put in place to ensure the team meets its overall goal. Examples of smaller goals could be: missing fewer than ten tackles per game or making more than five attacking line-breaks per game. If these smaller goals are met, it is more likely that the overall goal will be achieved.

**Mental preparation techniques** are used prior to a race, game, performance or competition, or just before the execution of a self-paced skill. The idea of mental preparation is that a person takes the time to get themselves into the right place psychologically, before they embark on the performance itself.

The four main mental preparation techniques are imagery, mental rehearsal, selective attention and positive thinking.

Often, an advanced performer, who is used to using mental preparation, will blend these four techniques into a routine that allows them to relax, focus, block out distraction and harness positivity. Most examples of a person using mental preparation will usually, therefore, use more than one technique.

## Imagery

Imagery is a technique used to combat stress, pressure and nerves. Being nervous or overexcited is completely natural, but can lead to poor performance because your body behaves differently when it is under stress. Your heart rate increases and your muscles tense, both of which make it harder for you to perform at your best.

Imagery involves performers imagining themselves in a relaxed place, in which they feel completely calm and relaxed in the moments before a performance. This could be, for example, a sunny beach or a familiar training environment. In a pressured scenario, like a diving or gymnastics final, it can be helpful to a performer to imagine that they are somewhere where no one is watching and they are completely at ease.

Performers who use the imagery technique say that they are calmer, more in control and better able to focus on the performance ahead.

> **Key term**
>
> **Mental preparation techniques:** A group of techniques, including imagery, mental rehearsal, selective attention and positive thinking, which are carried out before a performance. They take place within the mind of the performer, without any actual physical movement.

> **Study tip**
>
> As with anything, mental preparation techniques require practice. The more you have a go, the better you will get. Your imagery and mental rehearsal will be more detailed and vivid, while your ability to block out distractions, focus and approach the task ahead with positivity will improve.

◀ Imagery allows a performer to stay relaxed ahead of a performance that they may be nervous about.

123

## Mental rehearsal

Mental rehearsal is a technique that involves a performer practising a skill in their head before physically executing it. Rehearsing the perfect execution of the skill in their mind's eye reminds them of the key technical points that lead to success. Mental rehearsal is a mental trial run, which gives a performer an opportunity to practise a movement when physically practising it is not allowed. Many rugby goal kickers, triple jumpers, divers, golfers and basketball free-throw shooters use mental rehearsal to increase their focus and ensure that their skill execution is consistent.

▶ Performers like Owen Farrell, who have mastered the technique of mental rehearsal, are able to experience the feelings of muscles contracting and movements taking place without physically moving.

## Selective attention

Selective attention is a technique that involves actively blocking out distractions and focusing all concentration on the performance ahead. By directing their attention only to relevant information, the performer is in the zone and they are more likely to perform the skills and strategies that will lead to success.

◀ Some performers, like Laura Kenny, use music as part of a routine involving selective attention. Using the same playlist regularly creates feelings of familiarity, which can help the performer to focus.

## Positive thinking

As part of a mental preparation routine, it is important to be confident and positive. Approaching a performance with a 'can do' attitude and not allowing negative thoughts to cloud their thinking is very important, if a performer is going to perform at their best.

Positive self-talk is a positive thinking technique. This is when performers talk to themselves, either in their heads or out loud, as a way of blocking out negative self-talk. Negative self-talk is when your inner voice makes you doubt your ability, and it often occurs just before you take on a challenging task. Allowing negative thoughts to enter your mind at a crucial moment can distract you, upset your focus and contribute to a skill being poorly executed.

▶ As golfers like Justin Rose line up a putt and prepare for the shot, they must be confident that they will be successful. Doubt could make them tentative and prevent them sinking the putt.

## Activity

5  Carry out a mental preparation experiment:
   - Make sure everyone has a tennis ball, or a piece of screwed-up paper.
   - Stand, or sit in a circle, around a central bin or bucket. Take it in turns to practise throwing the ball into the bin a few times, so that you get a feel for it.
   - Split the group in half, ensuring that both halves have a mixture of people who are good at the task and people who are weaker at the task. Half will be the 'go' group and half will be the 'mentally prepare and go when you're ready' group.
   - On an instruction, each member of the 'go' group will quickly, without time to think, throw their ball into the bin, one after the other. How many balls go in?
   - Next, on a second instruction, the 'mentally prepare and go when you're ready' group will take it in turns to do just that. Each person should look at the target, take a few seconds to imagine they are somewhere calm and relaxing (imagery), run through the skill in their head and feel the action of throwing the ball into the bin (mental rehearsal), banish any distractions by concentrating exclusively on the task (selective attention), convince themselves that it will go in (positive thinking) and then throw. How many balls go in?

**Guidance** is the information given to someone to help them develop a skill, to improve and optimise their performance. There are four types of guidance:

 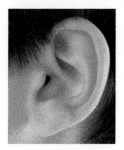  

▲ Visual guidance    ▲ Verbal guidance  ▲ Manual guidance      ▲ Mechanical guidance

The type of guidance used will depend on the skills being developed, and on the performers who are involved in the session.

## Visual guidance

**Visual guidance** is when guidance is presented in a form that the performer can look at. It can include anything from a live demonstration to a video or a film, a poster, a chart or court markings.

> ### Key terms
>
> **Guidance:** Information to aid the learning of a skill.
>
> **Visual guidance:** Information given to a performer to help them develop, which they can see. It involves demonstrations.

◀ Visual guidance: A coach or higher-level performer demonstrates basketball shooting skills to a group of young players.

When using visual guidance, it is important that the technique being shown is of good quality. It is also important that those learning watch closely and pay attention to the key points.

### Advantages
✓ Useful for all levels of performer.

✓ Especially good for young/inexperienced performers.

✓ Vision is most people's dominant sense.

✓ Allows performers to see what is required.

✓ Specific aspects of a whole skill can be observed.

✓ Performers can copy what they have seen.

### Disadvantages
✗ Demonstration or image must be of good quality.

✗ Some skills are too complex to demonstrate.

✗ Not effective if performers are not paying attention.

# Verbal guidance

**Verbal guidance** is when a coach explains how to perform a skill or tells a performer something.

▲ Verbal guidance: Coaches talk to performers and explain what is being done well and how they can improve.

## Key term

**Verbal guidance:** Information given to a performer to help them develop that is spoken to them and that they listen to. It involves the coach explaining the skill.

## Activity

6   Think about the last PE lesson you had, or the last training session you were involved in. What types of guidance did your teacher or coach use? Do you think these were the most appropriate for that session? Why?

## Advantages

✓ Especially useful for higher-level performers.

✓ Good way of highlighting key teaching points.

✓ Useful for sharing basic information and instructions.

✓ Questioning can often make a performer think.

## Disadvantages

✗ Can result in 'information overload'.

✗ Can be boring.

✗ Sports arenas are often noisy.

✗ Complex techniques/actions are often difficult to explain.

## Manual guidance

**Manual guidance** involves a coach physically moving a performer into the correct position, or supporting them as they perform a skill.

▲ Manual guidance: A coach will move a performer into the correct position so they can feel how the skill is meant to feel when done correctly.

### Advantages

✓ Good for complete beginners.

✓ Allows some development of correct feel.

### Disadvantages

✗ A movement can feel different when someone else is moving your body for you.

✗ Performer may not think that they're actually performing it themselves.

## Mechanical guidance

**Mechanical guidance** takes place when equipment is used to assist in the coaching process. This could take the form of floats in swimming or harnesses in diving, gymnastics and trampolining.

◀ Mechanical guidance: Equipment is used to allow complex skills to be performed safely or to build confidence.

### Activity

7 Discuss which types of guidance you might use if you were teaching/coaching the following performers, and how your chosen type of guidance would benefit the performer:
  a) a beginner in badminton
  b) a beginner in gymnastics
  c) a local club-level footballer
  d) a local club-level netballer
  e) an advanced triple jumper
  f) an advanced golfer.

### Advantages

✓ Good for teaching potentially dangerous skills.

✓ Can allow performer to gain a feel for a movement without fear.

✓ Good for building confidence.

### Disadvantages

✗ Equipment may be expensive.

✗ Performer can come to rely on the aid.

**Feedback** is information a performer receives about their performance. It helps them to develop and improve. Feedback can come during a performance or after its completion, as well as from the feelings the performer experiences or information passed to them by a coach.

Types of feedback include:

## Key term

**Feedback:** Information given to a performer during or after their performance, with the aim of improving future performances.

**① Intrinsic feedback**

Feedback a performer receives about their performance from within. How a movement feels, known as kinaesthesis, is an example of intrinsic feedback.

**② This is useful because:**

Performers, especially experienced performers, can respond immediately to intrinsic feedback. They can make adjustments during the performance and do not need to consult a coach. For example, a high diver may feel the need to tuck tighter during a dive because they are rotating too slowly.

**③ However:**

It requires a lot of experience to identify accurately what is going well, or went well, and what did not go so well. Intrinsic feedback is, therefore, unlikely to be of help to beginners.

**① Extrinsic feedback**

Feedback a performer receives about their performance from an outside source, like a coach.

**② This is useful because:**

Performers, especially inexperienced performers, will need someone else to tell them what went well and what needs adjusting next time. For example, a young gymnast may need to be told to straighten their legs and point their toes. Experienced performers can combine extrinsic feedback with intrinsic feedback to gain a full understanding of their performance.

**③ However:**

Extrinsic feedback is only useful if it is accurate and coming from someone who is knowledgeable. Experienced coaches are not always available to beginners.

**③ However:**

It can be challenging to break a whole performance down into its component parts. Also, experienced performers will need very detailed feedback, which will require a highly knowledgeable coach.

**① Knowledge of performance**

Feedback a performer receives about the quality of the skill execution and the performance process.

**② This is useful because:**

By focusing on the elements of the performance that went well and the elements that did not go as well as they could, the performer can develop an understanding of their strengths and weaknesses, and can identify what they need to do to improve. Improving elements of the performance will, ultimately, result in a better overall performance. For example, a rugby player may have passed the ball well during a match but missed too many tackles.

**① Knowledge of results**

Feedback on a performer's finishing position in a tournament or the time it took them to complete a race.

**② This is useful because:**

It gives the performer a quick and simple measure of their success. For example, a sprinter will know, very quickly, that they ran the 100 metres in a personal best time and finished third.

**③ However:**

Focusing on knowledge of results can be demotivating if a performer has not done as well as they had hoped. Only one person can win and it can be easy for performers who do not win to overlook the positive aspects of their own performance. Performers who do win might be tempted to focus on their win and ignore weaknesses in their performance that need improving.

**① Positive feedback**

Feedback about what a performer has done well in a performance.

**② This is useful because:**

Performers are motivated by positive feedback, especially beginners. It allows performers to acknowledge that certain aspects of their performance were successful, regardless of result. For example, a young golfer can receive positive feedback about their driving, irrespective of how their short game was.

**③ However:**

Positive feedback can overly emphasise the positive aspects of the performance and leave the performer feeling that they do not need to develop further.

**① Negative feedback**

Feedback about what a performer has not done well in a performance.

**② This is useful because:**

Negative feedback allows a coach to provide information on how the performance can be improved, which helps the performer prioritise specific elements in need of development in their training. For example, a swimmer being told that their turns and underwater sections were poor.

**③ However:**

It can become demoralising for performers if they hear too much negative feedback. Too many negative comments can also leave a performer not knowing which improvements to work on first.

**Study tip**

A performer can receive more than one type of feedback at once. However, issues can arise between a performer and their coach if they think differently about the performance, and if the feedback from different sources is conflicting.

**Activity**

8  Think back to the last time you participated in a sport or physical activity. What types of feedback were available to you? How useful was each type?

9  Consider the scenarios in activity 7 and discuss which types of feedback would be most beneficial to each performer.

# Practice questions

1 Which **one** of the following is a benefit of goal setting?

Put a tick (✓) in the box next to the correct answer.

A Makes you beat your personal best each time. ☐
B Increases motivation. ☐
C Means you do not need to train as often. ☐
D Decreases the effort you need. ☐

**[1]**

2 Which **one** of the following is **not** a characteristic of skilful movement?

Put a tick (✓) in the box next to the correct answer.

A Efficiency ☐
B Amazing ☐
C Co-ordinated ☐
D Aesthetic ☐

**[1]**

3 Which **one** of the following is the best example of a closed skill?

Put a tick (✓) in the box next to the correct answer.

A A volley in tennis. ☐
B Passing to a teammate in hockey. ☐
C Putting in golf. ☐
D An attacking header at goal in football. ☐

**[1]**

4 Which **one** of the following statements is an example of visual guidance?

Put a tick (✓) in the box next to the correct answer.

A Watching a video of an elite performer. ☐
B Having mini hurdles to jump over. ☐
C Having a coach hold your arm while
  you practice. ☐
D A coach shouting out instructions. ☐

**[1]**

5 Skills can be classified on a continuum from simple to complex.

Using an example, describe what makes a skill:

A simple **[2]**
B complex **[2]**

6 Give **two** practical examples of an open skill. **[2]**

7 Describe **two** mental preparation techniques. **[4]**

8 Compare knowledge of results with knowledge of performance. **[2]**

9 The SMART principle of goal setting suggests how goals should be written.

Describe the SMART principle of goal setting and discuss why using this principle is important. **[6]**

10 Different types of guidance are used to develop sporting performance.

Using practical examples, describe how two different types of guidance are used.

Explain which type of guidance is most suitable for beginners. **[6]**

# 2.3 Health, fitness and well-being

When you have worked through this chapter, you will have developed knowledge and understanding of:

- health, fitness and well-being
- diet and nutrition.

# Health and well-being

**Health** is a state of emotional, physical and social well-being.

People who are physically active, socially connected and emotionally content, will have high levels of **well-being**. They will be comfortable, healthy and happy. They are likely to live longer and lead more fulfilling lives. Health should, therefore, be the number one goal for all people.

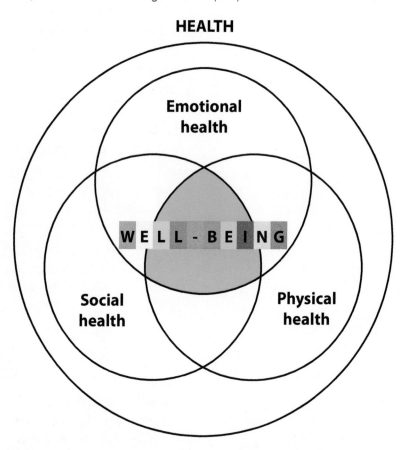

**HEALTH**

Emotional health

WELL - BEING

Social health

Physical health

In order to be healthy and well, people must make positive lifestyle choices. They must choose to:

- be active, ensuring that they can cope with the physical demands of their environment

- eat a healthy, balanced diet

- control their alcohol intake

- abstain from smoking and drug taking

- have a good work/life balance

- be socially connected

- think positively about the challenges they face.

---

## Key terms

**Health:** A state of emotional, physical and social well-being.

**Well-being:** A state of being comfortable, healthy and happy.

## Study tip

It is important to understand what 'health' and 'well-being' are separately, as well as to understand their relationship to one another.

## Activity

1  **a)** Create your own diagram, collage or poster that visually demonstrates the meanings of 'health' and 'well-being', and shows the relationship between them.

   **b)** Discuss your views on the importance of health and of well-being, and how a person can take positive steps to improve their general health and well-being.

## 2.3.2 The benefits of physical activity and the consequences of a sedentary lifestyle

**Fitness** is a person's ability to meet the physical demands placed on them by their environment. Regular **exercise** and **physical activity**, as part of an active lifestyle, improves a person's fitness and their physical health, and their general well-being as a result. In contrast, living a **sedentary lifestyle**, with little or no physical activity, and being unfit, can negatively affect a person's health and well-being. While fitness cannot guarantee full physical health, as illness and disease can affect anyone, being fit makes the body better able to cope with the demands placed on it, and reduces the risks of health problems associated with a sedentary lifestyle.

The benefits of physical activity on physical health are:

- improved components of fitness, making everyday tasks easier

- reduced risk of injury due to improved posture, increased bone density, and stronger ligaments, tendons and muscles

- healthy weight, and improved cardiovascular and respiratory efficiency, leading to reduced risk of health problems associated with a sedentary lifestyle.

### Key terms

**Fitness:** A person's ability to meet the physical demands placed on them by their environment.

**Exercise:** Activity that requires physical effort. It is usually carried out to sustain or bring about improvements to health and fitness.

**Physical activity:** Movement of the body by the skeletal muscles that requires energy expenditure.

**Sedentary lifestyle:** A lifestyle where there is little, irregular or no physical activity.

◀ Getting regular exercise, like swimming, brings improved fitness, which is a key factor in reducing the risk of health problems.

### Study tip

Fitness is broken down into separate components of fitness, which are described on pages 48–62. Depending on the types of exercise a person is involved in, different components of fitness will develop and contribute to their general fitness.

### Activity

2  **a)** The NHS provides guidelines for the amount of physical activity people of different ages need to do each week. Find out what the guidelines are, for children and for adults.

   **b)** Discuss how someone's job might impact on how likely they are to lead a sedentary lifestyle.

### Study tip

The physical health benefits of being fit link closely with the long-term training effects of exercise, which are discussed on pages 40–45.

## Physical health and the impact of a sedentary lifestyle

While being active and keeping fit can help to keep you physically healthy, a sedentary lifestyle is heavily associated with numerous long-term physical health issues.

### The physical consequences of a sedentary lifestyle

### Low level of fitness

People who live a sedentary lifestyle are not very active and, consequently, have very low levels of fitness. This means that tasks such as walking up stairs, playing with their children, or grandchildren, or running to catch a bus are difficult. People who get out of breath quickly and who suffer joint and muscle pain after performing simple activities will not enjoy their lives as much as people who are fitter.

### Increased risk of injury

People who are not very active will have weak ligaments and tendons, and less pliable muscles and joints with a reduced range of movement. People leading a sedentary lifestyle are, therefore, more likely to experience injuries, such as muscle strains and joint sprains, while taking part in everyday activities. Often, they will take longer to recover from injuries.

### Low bone density

Because people who live a sedentary lifestyle are not very active, they do not regularly stress their bones and their bones become less dense, weaker and more susceptible to fractures as a result. People living sedentary lifestyles are also more likely to develop osteoporosis, which is extremely low bone density that results in a very high risk of fracture.

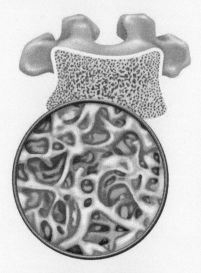

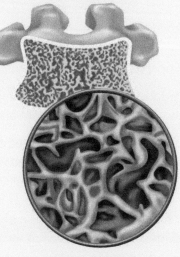

▲ The image at the top shows normal bone density. The image below shows osteoporosis.

### Poor posture

Spending too much time sitting, slouching at a desk and having weak core muscles can lead to poor posture. Poor posture creates extra pressure in the lower back and is likely to result in discomfort and pain. Pilates and yoga are examples of physical activities that develop core muscle strength and support the lower back, improving posture.

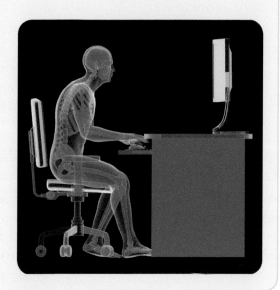

## Obesity

A person who leads a sedentary lifestyle and eats a high-calorie diet will put on weight, and may become obese. A person is obese if they weigh significantly more than the ideal weight for their height, and have an excess amount of body fat. A person is obese if they have a BMI (Body Mass Index) score of over 30. Being overweight or obese dramatically increases a person's chances of developing serious health complications, including coronary heart disease, high blood pressure and Type 2 diabetes. Physical activities, particularly high-intensity physical activities, such as HIIT and aerobics, burn a lot of calories and help people attain and maintain a healthy weight.

▶ A height–weight chart helps people to work out if they are the correct weight for their height. The NHS website (www.nhs.uk) also has an online BMI calculator.

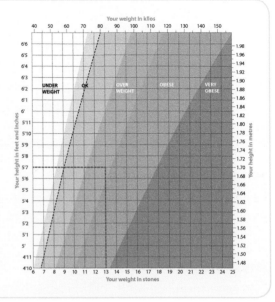

## High blood pressure

As fatty deposits accumulate in a person's blood vessels, as a result of living a sedentary lifestyle and eating a high-calorie diet, the lumens of the vessels become narrower. This makes it harder for blood to flow and causes high blood pressure or 'hypertension'. The heart then has to work harder to pump blood around the body, which can lead to other heart-related health problems. Physical activity, especially aerobic activity, helps combat this by expanding blood vessels and increasing blood flow, which prevents fatty deposits forming.

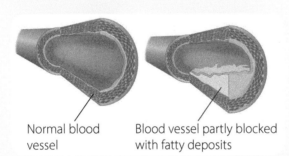

Normal blood vessel

Blood vessel partly blocked with fatty deposits

## Coronary heart disease (CHD)

The coronary artery is the blood vessel that supplies oxygenated blood to the muscle of the heart. Fatty deposits can narrow or block the lumen of the coronary artery and restrict or stop the supply of oxygen to the heart. This can result in angina (chest pain) and heart attack. Physical activity can help to prevent this by increasing the efficiency of the heart and maintaining higher cardiac output, thereby reducing the likelihood of fatty deposits forming.

## Type 2 diabetes

Insulin is a hormone produced by your body to convert carbohydrates into glucose. Type 2 diabetes occurs when your body does not produce enough insulin to function properly, or when your body does not react correctly to the insulin produced. The consequences of Type 2 diabetes can include blindness, kidney failure, heart attack and stroke. Being overweight or obese is one of the causes of Type 2 diabetes.

### Activity

3. You are concerned about the number of children in your local primary school who are overweight. In small groups, discuss what you could do to educate a Year 4 class about the dangers of a sedentary lifestyle, and to encourage them to be more physically active.

# Emotional health

Emotional health is crucial to a person's general well-being. Being self-confident, comfortable with your appearance, self-aware and resilient are very important in helping you to cope with the challenges life brings. People with poor emotional health may suffer from anxiety and depression, worrying more than normal and thinking they are worthless and have little to offer. Being involved in physical activity and sport can improve a person's emotional health.

### Self-esteem and confidence

Developing components of fitness, achieving goals and, potentially, sporting success helps to increase confidence and improve self-esteem.

### Stress management

Exercise releases hormones, called endorphins, which help to combat stress. In addition, looking forward to taking part in physical activity and sport can stimulate positive thoughts and help to balance less enjoyable aspects of life.

### Image

Losing weight, gaining muscle tone and feeling more physically active can improve body image and make people feel more content within themselves.

# Social health

Socially healthy people are able to form and maintain good relationships with others. This does not mean they never have disagreements, but they are able to communicate effectively to avoid or resolve disputes. A socially healthy person is also sensitive to the needs of the people around them, and can adapt to different social situations. Taking part in physical activity and sport can improve a person's social health.

### Friendship

Whether attending exercise classes, joining a sports team or meeting existing friends to play sport recreationally, taking part in physical activity provides lots of opportunities to meet new people, make new friends and develop bonds that can last a lifetime.

### Belonging to a group

Being part of a team or a club can give you a sense of belonging, as you work together to achieve a common goal and develop your teamwork skills.

### Loneliness

When people are socially active, have friends and feel that they belong, they are less likely to feel lonely and isolated, which is one of the most common triggers for depression.

# Health, fitness and well-being for different age groups

People have different priorities at different stages of their lives and, over time, a person's relationship with physical activity is likely to change. As the level at which they engage in physical activity changes, its impact on their health, fitness and well-being will also change.

## Age group: 5–18-year-olds

Between the ages of five and 18, young people are in full-time education. The majority do not have many responsibilities outside of school and, therefore, if they choose to, most have the time to participate in sport and physical activity, and socialise with their friends. Parents, guardians and schools should be making sure that all young people eat a balanced diet and do not start smoking or drinking alcohol. As a result, it is hoped that most young people will be healthy, and have a sense of well-being.

However, advances in technology mean that many young people are now able to interact with others at a distance and, therefore, spend much more time alone than children who grew up before use of the internet was widespread. Using social media and gaming are sedentary pastimes, which means that young people today are less active than they were in the past. This trend has brought a rise in emotional, physical and social problems.

**Study tip**

A person's changing relationship with physical activity over time is one of the factors affecting participation in physical activity and sport. For more information on the factors affecting participation, see pages 91–97.

**Activity** — DATA

4 This graph shows the percentage of children who were overweight, by age group, between 1994 and 2013.
   a) Describe the trend for each year group between 1994 and 2013.
   b) Explain what the trend suggests about how the lifestyles of 2–5-year-olds have changed between 2003 and 2013?
   c) Predict the percentage of children who will be overweight, by age group, in 2020.

## Age group: 19–39-year-olds

As a person enters adulthood they take on more responsibilities. They go to university, or start work, and they may move away from their parents' home and have children of their own. They will have less disposable income and less free time. Those who were active in their youth will often find the time and money to continue to participate in sport and physical activity, and will continue to experience the emotional, physical and social benefits of participation. In contrast, those who were not very active in their youth will find it difficult to prioritise physical activity.

## Age group: 40–64-year-olds

As people reach this period of their lives, their enthusiasm for sport and physical activity can wane. This age group experiences many barriers to participation, and there is a drop in the number of people in their 40s, 50s and early 60s engaging in sport and physical activity. However, those who do manage to stay physically active will experience significant emotional, physical and social benefits, which will do wonders for their health and well-being in later life.

## Age group: 65+

During retirement, many people find they have the free time and disposable income to take part in sport and physical activity. Unfortunately, those who have not developed a habit of participation throughout their lives will find they are faced with many barriers to participation. Some may also find health problems make it more difficult to participate.

However, those who do make the effort to take part in sport and physical activity will feel physically fitter, happier and more connected with their community. Older people can find themselves isolated and lonely if they outlive partners and friends, and joining a walking group or a fitness class can help them make new friends.

---

### Activity

5  **a)** What does the table show?

   **b)** Which age group has the highest level of activity and which age group has the highest level of inactivity?

   **c)** What trends do you notice when looking at the inactive and active columns?

| Age | Inactive (<30 minutes per week) | | Fairly active (30–149 minutes per week) | | Active (150+ minutes per week) | |
|---|---|---|---|---|---|---|
| | **Population total** | **Rate (%)** | **Population total** | **Rate (%)** | **Population total** | **Rate (%)** |
| 16–24 | 878,700 | 14.1% | 599,000 | 9.7% | 4,710,200 | 76.2% |
| 25–34 | 1,329,800 | 17.6% | 962,600 | 12.9% | 5,190,400 | 69.5% |
| 35–44 | 1,289,500 | 18.0% | 948,000 | 13.4% | 4,867,100 | 68.6% |
| 45–54 | 1,465,300 | 18.9% | 1,015,200 | 13.2% | 5,217,600 | 67.9% |
| 55–64 | 1,457,400 | 23.4% | 796,400 | 12.9% | 3,930,200 | 63.7% |
| 65–74 | 1,319,600 | 24.8% | 680,500 | 12.9% | 3,287,300 | 62.3% |
| 75+ | 2,024,800 | 45.4% | 596,400 | 13.5% | 1,815,200 | 41.1% |

*Source: Sport England*, Active Lives Survey 2015–2016

Making sure you have the right nutrition for health and growth by eating a healthy, **balanced diet** is an essential part of a healthy lifestyle. The 'Eatwell' guide has been developed to inform people of the proportions of different food groups they should eat. Following this guidance guarantees that you will consume the right proportion of all seven components of a healthy, balanced diet: carbohydrates, proteins, fats, vitamins, minerals, fibre and water.

## Key term

**Balanced diet:** A diet that contains the correct proportions of carbohydrates, proteins, fats, vitamins, minerals, fibre and water necessary to maintain good health.

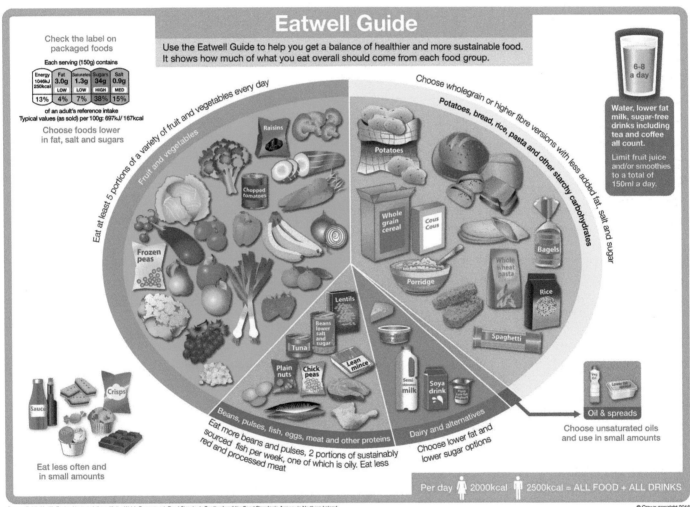

### Eatwell Guide

Use the Eatwell Guide to help you get a balance of healthier and more sustainable food. It shows how much of what you eat overall should come from each food group.

Source: Public Health England in association with the Welsh Government, Food Standards Scotland and the Food Standards Agency in Northern Ireland

© Crown copyright 2016

Everyone who takes part in physical activity and sport should eat a balanced diet to ensure their bodies are prepared to cope with the demands placed on them. But, as we shall see, some performers have slightly different dietary requirements, which relate to the components of fitness they need to achieve and the training they do.

## Study tip

Remember that the 'Eatwell' guide gives guidance on food groups, so that people can put balanced meals together. Food groups contain the different components of a diet. For example, foods in the potatoes, bread, rice and pasta group contain lots of carbohydrates; and foods in the beans, pulses, fish, eggs and meat group contain lots of protein.

# Carbohydrates

Carbohydrates are the main source of energy for the body. They are stored in the body as glycogen and, when we exercise, it is broken down into glucose, which provides the working muscles with energy. When supplies of glucose become depleted, less energy is released and a performer becomes fatigued. It is critical that someone taking part in physical activity and sport consumes enough carbohydrates to fuel their work.

## Types of carbohydrate

There are two types of carbohydrate. Each type is contained in different foods and releases energy at a different rate:

1 Simple sugars. These break down quickly and provide a burst of energy, which can be useful just before a training session or a race. Snacks and gel pouches consumed during events are likely to contain simple sugars.

2 Complex starches. These break down and release energy slowly, making them an ideal source of energy for endurance performers. Pasta and rice will be a staple of an endurance performer's weekly diet plan.

## Carbohydrate intake for different needs

- Normal needs: 50–60 per cent of the diet of a person who does a normal amount of activity, as part of an active lifestyle, should consist of carbohydrates. These should be mainly complex starches.

- Endurance performer's needs: 60–70 per cent of the diet of an endurance performer in training should consist of carbohydrates. Again, these should be mainly complex starches. This is because an endurance performer needs more energy to fuel their higher activity levels.

Endurance performers need to enter a competition with a large store of glycogen to fuel their bodies during the race, and to allow them to work for longer before suffering from fatigue. They, therefore, use a strategy known as 'carbohydrate loading'. This involves a performer increasing the proportion of carbohydrates in their diet in the lead-up to competition, to increase their store of glycogen.

▶ People who are training for a marathon will need to increase their carbohydrate intake, especially in the lead-up to the race.

▲ Simple sugars are found in sweets, honey, fruit juice, chocolate, jam and yogurt.

▲ Complex starches are found in bread, pasta, rice and oatmeal.

# Protein

Protein provides the body with amino acids. These are the building blocks of all human cells, controlling many vital processes, and are essential for muscle growth and repair.

## Protein intake for different needs

- Normal needs: 0.8 grams of protein per kilogram of body weight will support growth and repair for someone involved in a normal amount of activity, as part of an active lifestyle. This can easily be gained from a normal, healthy, balanced diet.

- Strength and power performers' needs: 1.2–1.5 grams of protein per kilogram of body weight is needed by strength and power performers to enable them to increase their muscle mass. The combination of weight training and an increase in protein will result in hypertrophy of muscles and an increase in strength. This is a fairly substantial increase in protein, and it should only be consumed as part of a carefully designed diet plan.

▲ Meat, fish, eggs, pulses, beans and nuts are good sources of protein.

## Study tip

The need for increased protein when strength training links closely to the long-term training effects of exercise on muscles, which are explained on pages 40–42.

## Activity

6   In pairs, plan two meals, consisting of just main courses, for two athletes. One of you should plan a meal for an endurance performer, while the other plans a meal for a strength performer. Before you start, discuss how the two meals will differ, and include pictures in your presentation. Remember to design meals that people will actually want to eat!

▲ Strength and power performers will often consume additional protein in the form of protein shakes. Foods that are rich in protein, like meat, are also relatively high in fats, and strength and power performers in training do not want to eat too much fat.

## Fats

Fats are an essential part of a healthy diet. Consuming fats doesn't make you fat; it is consuming more calories than you burn off that will make you gain weight. Fats are an important source of energy. They are also important for transporting fat-soluble vitamins around the body, and certain fatty acids are vital for good health.

### Types of fat

There are two main types of fat:

- saturated fats, which are typically solid at room temperature. Too much saturated fat in a diet increases the risk of developing heart disease, so consumption of foods containing saturated fats should be limited

- unsaturated fats, which are normally liquid at room temperature. They are much healthier for you than saturated fats, and play a role in reducing the risk of developing heart disease.

Fats are a very good source of energy but it takes a relatively long time to convert fat into energy. This can be useful if you are involved in high-level endurance training. However, someone who has a high fat diet and does not train hard will put on weight.

▲ Saturated fats are found in fatty meat, butter, cheese, cakes, crisps and biscuits.

▲ Unsaturated fats are found in oily fish, nuts, olive oil, sunflower oil and avocado.

## Vitamins

Vitamins play an important role in ensuring that vital chemical reactions take place in the body. For example, Vitamins B3 and B6 help gas exchange to take place. Vitamins are also responsible for making sure that essential bodily functions happen, including blood production and hormone regulation.

### Types of vitamins

There are two types of vitamins:

- fat-soluble vitamins, which are stored in fatty tissue and called on when needed: Vitamin A, Vitamin D, Vitamin E, Vitamin K and Beta-carotene

- water-soluble vitamins, which generally cannot be stored and must be replenished every day: Vitamin C, the six B vitamins, biotin and folic acid.

◀ Vitamins are found in fruits, vegetables, dairy products, oily fish, beans, seeds and nuts.

▶ Vitamin D is produced in the body when your skin is exposed to sunlight. It is crucial for healthy bones, which all sports performers need. Some athletes, who largely train indoors, may need to take supplements to ensure that they are not deficient in Vitamin D.

## Minerals

Minerals play an essential role in almost all bodily functions. To function properly, the body needs a wide range of minerals, including calcium, fluoride, iron, magnesium, phosphorous and potassium. For example, calcium is found in strong, healthy bones, and iron plays an important part in releasing energy.

◀ Minerals are found in all kinds of different foods. For example, shellfish, almonds and watercress are good sources of iron.

▶ Minerals, including potassium and sodium, can be lost through sweat during exercise. Some sports drinks contain minerals and drinking them after physical activity can help you to replenish the losses.

## Activity

7 Research two vitamins and two minerals and prepare a fact sheet about each of them. For each one, identify:
- what foods it is found in
- what it does
- why it is especially important for a sportsperson.

## Fibre

Fibre is the name given to the indigestible parts of food, and it is essential for healthy bowel function. It helps your body absorb vital nutrients as well as remove waste products by providing the bulk that is needed to move them through your digestive system. Fibre also makes you feel fuller for longer so that you eat less and are better able to maintain your optimum weight.

It is important for performers to start their day with a healthy breakfast that is rich in fibre because it helps the body stay in peak condition.

▲ Fruit, vegetables, brown bread, bran and wholegrain cereals are all high in fibre.

# Water and hydration

Sixty per cent of the human body is made up of water, so taking in water as part of a balanced diet, is essential to maintaining appropriate levels of **hydration**. When a person is hydrated they have enough water in their body for it to function properly. However, if a person suffers from **dehydration**, their body does not contain enough water and does not function as efficiently as it should.

Water keeps joints lubricated.

Water carries vitamins and minerals around the body.

Water aids digestion and helps to prevent constipation.

**The role of water**

Water helps to remove waste products from the body through urine.

Water keeps blood fluid, so that it flows around the body easily.

Water helps to regulate body temperature through sweating.

## Water intake

The average recommended daily intake of water is 2 litres (4 pints) and this is sufficient under normal circumstances. However, a person needs more water to maintain hydration when they are involved in sport and physical activity, because water is lost through sweat. Depending on the intensity and duration of the activity, as well as the weather conditions, a person may need to increase their fluid intake quite considerably, in order to stay properly hydrated.

Dehydration prevents the body from functioning properly. It results in:

- thirst

- decreased skill level

- increased body temperature, which can cause the body to overheat

- muscle fatigue, often leading to cramping

- increased heart rate, as the heart has to work harder to pump thicker blood around the body

- slower reaction time

- dizziness, nausea, blurred vision and headaches

- death (in very extreme cases).

**Activity**

8   Keep a food diary for a week, writing down or using an app to log everything that you eat and drink. Then use your diary to answer the following questions:

a)   Is your diet balanced? Explain your answer, remembering to think about all seven components of a healthy, balanced diet.

b)   What do you need to add or remove from your diet to make it balanced?

▲ During a marathon, runners must rehydrate regularly to ensure that they can complete the race safely.

# Practice questions

1 Which **one** of the following is a consequence of a sedentary lifestyle?
Put a tick (✔) in the box next to the correct answer.
A Weight gain. ☐
B Good quality sleep. ☐
C Improved fitness. ☐
D High energy levels. ☐

**[1]**

2 Which **one** of the following describes the role of fat in a balanced diet?
Put a tick (✔) in the box next to the correct answer.
A It helps gas exchange. ☐
B It provides the body with amino acids. ☐
C It is a source of fuel. ☐
D It ensures adequate hydration. ☐

**[1]**

3 Which **one** of the following is the major symptom of osteoporosis?
Put a tick (✔) in the box next to the correct answer.
A Chest pain. ☐
B High blood pressure. ☐
C Being underweight. ☐
D Lots of bone fractures. ☐

**[1]**

4 Which **one** of the following statements describes how participation in physical activity can increase emotional well-being?
Put a tick (✔) in the box next to the correct answer.
A It provides opportunities to socialise. ☐
B It increases self-esteem. ☐
C It helps to avoid obesity. ☐
D It increases stroke volume. ☐

**[1]**

5 Give one reason why each of these components of a balanced diet is important.
A Vitamins
B Fibre **[2]**

6 Describe coronary heart disease (CHD). **[2]**

7 People over the age of 65 benefit from engaging in physical activity. Give one example of a benefit of physical activity for a person over the age of 65 on:
A emotional health **[1]**
B social health. **[1]**

8 This table shows activity levels for different groups of people according to their employment status:

| Working status | Inactive (<30 minutes per week) | | Fairly active (30–149 minutes per week) | | Active (150+ minutes per week) | |
|---|---|---|---|---|---|---|
| | Population total | Rate (%) | Population total | Rate (%) | Population total | Rate (%) |
| Working full or part time | 5,315,100 | 20.2% | 3,707,400 | 14.2% | 17,723,900 | 65.6% |
| Unemployed | 438,500 | 31.4% | 193,700 | 13.2% | 939,700 | 55.4% |
| Not working (e.g. retired, looking after children) | 5,046,200 | 38.5% | 1,889,700 | 14.7% | 6,228,400 | 46.7% |
| Student full or part time | 242,800 | 12.7% | 174,800 | 9.2% | 1,542,800 | 78.1% |
| Other working status | 304,300 | 33.0% | 115,700 | 12.7% | 518,400 | 54.3% |

*Source: Sport England*, Active Lives Survey November 2015–2016

A Identify the group with the highest activity levels. **[1]**

B Give **one** reason as to why those 'not working' may have the lowest activity level. **[1]**

9 Fitness plays a key role in a person's physical health. Explain the benefits of physical activity to a person's physical health.
Why can fitness not guarantee that a person will have good physical health? **[6]**

10 Carbohydrates and protein are two components of a balanced diet.
Explain the role of carbohydrates and protein.
Why do these two components of a balanced diet have a different level of importance for different types of sports performer? **[6]**

When you have worked through this chapter, you will have developed knowledge and understanding of:

- what is required for the practical performance component of the course (30 per cent of your overall grade)

- what is required for the analysing and evaluating performance task (10 per cent of your overall grade).

This component assesses your performance in three different physical activities throughout your course. Your total mark is worth 30 per cent of your overall grade.

You must choose **three** activities from the list provided by OCR.
You must choose:

- one team activity

- one individual activity

- one activity of your choice, either team or individual.

It is important to know where your strengths currently lie, and to use this information to think about possible combinations of physical activities. However, while it is a good idea to have thought about your possible combinations, it is sensible not to rule other activities out. You may surprise yourself and end up with a different combination that earns you more marks.

If one or more of the activities on your list of three possible options is not delivered at school, you must plan ahead and work out when and how you will gain video evidence of your performance. You should speak to your PE teacher about this.

▲ For example, you could combine netball (team activity), singles tennis (individual activity) and football (choice). This kind of combination would obviously suit a good games player.

▲ For example, you could combine doubles badminton (team activity), swimming (individual activity) and dance (choice). This kind of combination would suit someone who excels in more individualised activities.

For each activity, you will be assessed on:

- your range of skills
- the quality of those skills
- your physical attributes
- your decision-making.

It is very likely that your teacher will assess you in many more than three activities to allow you to find your highest scoring combination. This means you should try your very best in every activity in every lesson, to ensure that the marks you receive, across the four areas of criteria, demonstrate your full potential. Every extra mark will increase your chance of achieving the grade you want overall.

At the end of the course, you may be selected to attend moderation. This means that the marks given by your teachers are checked to ensure they line up with the marks given by other teachers at other schools for performances of similar quality. If you are selected to be moderated, it is imperative that you do your very best.

---

## Activity

1  **a)**  Look through the lists of team and individual activities in OCR's *Guide to Non-exam Assessment (NEA)* and consider which activities you are actively involved in on a regular basis.

   **b)**  Think back to Key Stage 3 and reflect on your performance in activities you had access to then. Which activities did you improve in most over the three years? Which did you enjoy most? Which did you find most challenging?

   **c)**  Find out from your teacher whether there are likely to be any new activities offered in Key Stage 4 in which you might perform well.

   **d)**  Look at the assessment criteria for the activities you are considering, and check that the combinations you are thinking about are allowed.

   **e)**  With the help of your peers and teachers, create several possible combinations that could allow you to access the highest possible number of marks.

# 3.2 Analysing and evaluating performance (AEP)

This component assesses your ability to analyse and evaluate your practical performance, or the practical performance of a peer. Having selected the practical activity from the OCR list that you are most comfortable with, you will be given 14 hours to complete this task.

Before you begin, your teacher will run a task induction session, where the requirements of the task will be outlined to you. Be sure to ask any questions at this point.

The task requires you to:

- analyse aspects of the practical performance
- evaluate the strengths and weaknesses of the performance
- produce an action plan, which aims to improve the quality and effectiveness of the performance.

This task is designed to assess your knowledge of your chosen practical activity, as well as your ability to apply elements of theory that you have learned through the theory components of the course.

## Who will you analyse?

When selecting someone to analyse, you will need to consider the following:

- Are you more comfortable analysing yourself or someone else?
- Does the performer you have in mind display a suitable number of strengths and weaknesses in your chosen activity?
- Do you have access to the performer you have in mind? If you decide to analyse someone else, they will need to be in your class.

**Study tip**

If you have access arrangements, such as extra time or use of a laptop, double check that your teacher has factored this in to the task.

**Study tip**

Throughout your theory lessons, you will be encouraged to apply the theory you are learning to practical activities. Consider using the practical activity you will choose for this task as much as possible, to help you prepare for this assessment.

> **(1) Testing the performer's components of fitness and identifying their physical strengths and weaknesses (2–3 hours)**
>
> First you must test the performer's components of fitness.
>
> Then, to identify the performer's physical strengths and weaknesses, you will need to compare the results of the performer's fitness tests with normative data. This includes the data in this book and any data you have previously collected.
>
> The components of fitness and how to test them are described on pages 48–62.

## ② Analysing the chosen physical activity and assessing the performer's strengths and weaknesses in relation to it (3–4 hours)

This part of the task can be broken down into three sections:

- analysing the importance of the different components of fitness in the chosen activity

- preparing an overview of the key skills in the activity

- assessing the performer's strengths and weaknesses against the components of fitness and key skills required for success in the chosen activity.

### Analysing the importance of the different components of fitness in the chosen activity

Every sport or physical activity requires a different combination of components of fitness for success. In order to analyse which components of fitness are important for your chosen activity, you could place all ten components of fitness in order, from the most important to the least important for your chosen activity, and provide examples to explain where each component of fitness is seen in the activity, and why it appears where it does in your order of importance.

### Preparing an overview of the key skills in the activity

List around six skills that are key in your chosen physical activity. OCR's *Guide to Non-exam Assessment (NEA)* provides lists of core and advanced skills for each activity, which you are likely to be familiar with. This information will help you with this task, but you will need to decide which are the 'key' skills.

Then, provide an overview of where and when each of the key skills is demonstrated within the physical activity and how effective execution can affect the overall performance.

### Assessing the performer's strengths and weaknesses against the components of fitness and key skills required for success in the chosen activity

Take your list of components of fitness required for success in your chosen activity. For each component, state whether you think the performer is strong or weak compared to the other components. Now justify your decision by explaining why you have come to this conclusion. Then do the same for the key skills required for success in your chosen activity.

Remember that it is highly likely that components of fitness will influence skill execution, so be sure to identify any links. For example, 'The performer's quadriceps are not very powerful, which affects their ability to jump for a rebound.'

▲ Why are these skills key in football? Tackling, for example, is hugely important because it breaks up opposition attacks and allows possession to be won.

**Study tip**

Use technical language wherever you can. For example, refer to quadriceps rather than thigh muscles.

## ③ Analysing a specific skill or technique in your chosen activity (1–2 hours)

This part of the task requires you to analyse a specific skill or technique from your chosen activity, thinking about:

- the movement involved (the joint involved and the types of movement available at that joint, as well as the muscles involved and the roles of those muscles)

- the classification of the skill (where it is on the difficulty continuum and where it is on the environmental continuum).

**Study tip**

Consider analysing the key skill that you have identified as your performer's biggest weakness. This will help you to write your action plan, and will make the whole task flow better.

◀ Having photographs of the skill you are analysing will help you.

The theory needed for this part of the task is covered on the following pages:

- types of synovial joints: page 9
- types of movement at joints: pages 10–11
- the location of major muscle groups: page 13
- the roles of muscles in movement: pages 14–15
- classification of skills: pages 117–119.

## Analysing the movement involved

Most skills involve many joints in the body so, depending on how fast you can work, you could focus on the most important part of the body. For example, if you are analysing a swimming stroke, you could focus on the arm action (shoulder, elbow) and not describe the leg kick (hip and knee). This said, the more detail you are able to provide in the time the better. Consult your teacher about how much you should try to do.

You could present your analysis in a table. For example:

**Skill: Badminton smash**

| Joint | Articulating bones | Movement | Muscle group | Muscle role | Fixator |
|-------|--------------------|----------|--------------|-------------|---------|
| Elbow | Humerus, radius, ulna | Extension | Triceps | Agonist | Deltoid |
| Elbow | Humerus, radius, ulna | Extension | Biceps | Antagonist | Deltoid |
|  |  |  |  |  |  |

## Classifying the skill

Place the chosen skill on the two continua that you have learned about:

difficulty continuum (simple ◄────► complex)

environmental continuum (open ◄────► closed).

Write a statement underneath justifying why you have placed the chosen skill in that position. What makes the skill more open than closed? Why is it not completely open? You could compare the skill to well-known examples from the extremes of the continua to help you do this. For example:

Open ◄──────────**X**──────────────► Closed

A badminton smash is more open than closed because the shot depends, to some extent, on the shot played by the opponent. Also, the placement of the smash depends on the opponent's position on the court. It is not completely open, however, because most smash shots are played under similar circumstances, which can be predicted and practised in a controlled environment. There is no wind and no one else involved in the shot itself.

## ④ Produce an action plan to improve an aspect of the performer's performance in the chosen activity (4–5 hours)

You can produce an action plan to improve **either** a skill **or** a component of fitness.

Start by stating what your action plan will develop and justifying why you have chosen to develop the skill or component of fitness you have selected. You need to make a link between the performer's strengths and weaknesses and what you have chosen to develop. Under most circumstances, you should focus on improving the performer's biggest weakness, so that improvements have a big impact on performance.

Next, discuss the theory that will impact the action plan:

- the SMART principle of goal setting that will be used to set goals (found on pages 121–122)

- the principles of training that have been considered in developing the action plan (found on pages 63–67)

- the way risks will be identified and minimised (found on pages 81–85).

Finally, you need to outline the drills and practices that you want the performer to carry out to improve the aspect of their performance that you have chosen. For each drill or practice, provide:

**1** a description of how the drill or practice is set up and works.

**2** coaching points that should be emphasised during the drill or practice.

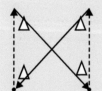 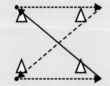 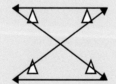 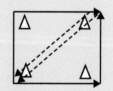

▲ Sketching a diagram to illustrate each drill or practice allows you to explain clearly how it is set up and works. You can then add your coaching points alongside. For example, 'Front foot must go to the pitch of the ball' would be a coaching point for a drive in cricket.

You should include around six drills or practices, which are progressive. This means that your action plan will start with a very simple drill or practice, which focuses on the skill in isolation. Then, each subsequent practice should get more complex, with, for example, more time pressure or more opposition. Your final practice will be almost a full performance, with conditions set to ensure that the skill being developed is used often. For example, you may set the following condition if your action plan is focusing on heading in football: 'You can only score with a header.'

### Study tip

Although you can produce an action plan to improve a skill or a component of fitness, the marking criteria refers to drills and practices. It may, therefore, be simplest to produce an action plan for a skill. If you decide to produce an action plan for a component of fitness, you will need to consider something that looks more like a training programme.

# Glossary

## A

**Abduction** Movement away from the midline of the body.

**Adaptation** A physical change that makes a body system more efficient.

**Adduction** Movement towards the midline of the body.

**Aerobic capacity** The greatest volume of oxygen that can be consumed and used by a person.

**Aerobic exercise** Working at a low to moderate intensity so that the body has time to use oxygen to release energy and can work for a continuous period of time. Long distance running is an example of aerobic exercise.

**Aerobic training zone** When a performer is working at 60–80 per cent of their maximum heart rate (MHR) they are working in the aerobic training zone. This means that they are working at a low enough intensity to allow oxygen to be used to release energy, but at a high enough intensity to achieve overload.

**Agility** The ability to change direction at speed; nimbleness.

**Agonist** The muscle that works to create a movement.

**Anaerobic exercise** Working at a high or very high intensity so that the body does not have time to use oxygen to release energy and can only work for a short period of time. Sprinting up a hill is an example of anaerobic exercise.

**Anaerobic training zone** When a performer is working at 80–90 per cent of their maximum heart rate (MHR) they are working in the anaerobic training zone.

**Antagonist** The muscle that works in the opposite way to the agonist, relaxing to allow movement.

**Antagonistic muscle action** A pair of muscles work together to produce movement, with one muscle contracting whilst the other muscle relaxes. For example, an antagonistic muscle action takes place in the upper arm as the biceps contracts and the triceps relaxes.

**Aorta** The artery that carries blood from the heart to the rest of the body.

**Arteries** Blood vessels that carry oxygenated blood from the heart to muscles and organs.

**Articulating bones** Bones that move relative to each other at a joint.

**Atria** This is the plural of "atrium". There are two atria in the heart. These are the upper chambers of the heart where blood enters.

**Axis** An imaginary line around which the body can turn. "Axes" is the plural of axis.

## B

**Balance** The ability to keep your body stable by maintaining your centre of mass above your base of support.

**Balanced diet** A diet that contains the correct proportions of carbohydrates, proteins, fats, vitamins, minerals, fibre and water necessary to maintain good health.

**Bicuspid valve** A one-way gate that separates the left atrium from the left ventricle.

**Blood vessel** A tubular structure that carries blood around our bodies.

**Bone density** The thickness and strength of bones.

**Breathing rate** The number of breaths taken in a minute. Also referred to as 'respiratory rate'.

## C

**Capillaries** Blood vessels that wrap around muscles and organs so that gas exchange can take place.

**Capilliarisation** An increase in the number of blood capillaries in the body. It is one of the long-term effects of exercise.

**Cardiac output** The volume of blood pumped out of the heart per minute.

**Cardiovascular endurance** The ability to release energy aerobically over a long period of time. It is also referred to as stamina.

**Cardiovascular-respiratory system** The name given to the combined body system that involves your cardiac, vascular and respiratory systems. These are usually combined when discussing oxygen delivery.

**Cartilage** A tough, elastic, fibrous connective tissue that prevents friction at a joint.

**Circuit training** A series of exercises performed one after another at stations, which focus on different muscle groups.

**Circumduction** A circular movement at a joint that combines flexion, extension, abduction and adduction.

**Class of lever** The type of lever. There are first class, second class and third class levers.

**Closed skill** A skill that is performed in a predictable environment. For example, a player throwing into a line-out in rugby.

**Commercialisation** The management or exploitation of a person, organisation or activity in a way designed to make a profit.

**Complex skill** A skill that requires a lot of focus and decision-making to perform. For example, a twisting somersault.

**Continuous training** Training that involves working a steady intensity with no rest intervals. It can be performed at any intensity within the aerobic training zone.

**Cool down** Less strenuous exercises, following on from more intense activity, where physiological activity is allowed to gradually return to normal resting levels.

**Co-ordination** The ability to move different body parts together effectively.

**Culture** The ideas, customs and social behaviour of a particular social group.

# D

**Dehydration** Not having the appropriate level of water in the body for it to function optimally.

**Deoxygenated blood** Blood containing a low concentration of oxygen.

**Deviance** Behaviour that is either unethical, immoral or seriously breaks the rules and norms of a sport.

**Diffusion** The process of a gas moving from an area of high partial pressure to an area of low partial pressure.

**Discrimination** The unfair treatment of categories of people. When people are discriminated against, they often do not have the same opportunities as categories of people who are not discriminated against.

**Duration** How long an activity lasts for.

# E

**Effort** The source of the energy. For example, muscles in the body.

**Effort arm** The distance from the fulcrum to the effort.

**Energy** The capacity to do work.

**Ethnicity** Describes the ethnic group you belong to. An ethnic group is a social group that shares cultural traditions, a religion, a language or other factors.

**Exercise** Activity that requires physical effort. It is usually carried out to sustain or bring about improvements to health and fitness.

**Extension** The angle at a joint increases as a limb straightens.

# F

**Fartlek training** Training that varies in intensity, consisting of different length bursts of highly intense work alternating with activity of lower intensity.

**Feedback** Information given to a performer during or after their performance, with the aim of improving future performances.

**Fitness** A person's ability to meet the physical demands placed on them by their environment.

**FITT** The acronym FITT describes the key components of an effective exercise programme:

- Frequency – the number of times training takes place
- Intensity – how hard the training is
- Time – how long you train for
- Type – the method of training used.

**Fixator** A muscle that acts as a stabiliser, helping the agonist to work effectively to create movement.

**Flexibility** The range of movement available around a joint.

**Flexion** The angle at a joint decreases as a limb bends.

**Frontal axis of rotation** An imaginary line passing horizontally through the body from front to back. A gymnast performing a cartwheel moves around this axis.

**Frontal plane** An imaginary line that divides the body from front to back vertically.

**Fulcrum** A fixed pivot point. For example, a joint in the body.

**Functions of the skeleton** The skeleton performs six important functions. These are: support, posture, protection, movement, blood cell production and storage of minerals.

# G

**Gamesmanship** Where the laws of the game are interpreted in ways, which while not illegal, are not in the spirit of the game; pushing the limits to gain an unfair advantage.

**Gas exchange** The movement of gases that takes place at the alveoli and capillaries.

**Goal setting** The process of setting targets that a performer will work towards achieving.

**The golden triangle** A graphic representation of the interdependent relationship between sponsorship, sporting events and the media.

**Guidance** Information to aid the learning of a skill.

# H

**Health** A state of emotional, physical and social well-being.

**Heart rate** The number of times the heart beats per minute.

**High intensity interval training (HIIT)** Training that involves alternating between periods of very intense work in the anaerobic training zone and periods of active recovery in the aerobic training zone.

**Hydration** Having the appropriate level of water in the body for it to function optimally.

**Hypertrophy** The increase in size of skeletal or cardiac muscle.

# I

**Intensity** How hard you work.

**Interval training** Training that incorporates periods of exercise and periods of rest.

# L

**Lactic acid** A waste product that builds up in the muscles when a person performs anaerobically. A build-up of lactic acid causes muscle fatigue and pain.

**Lever** A rigid bar or object that moves around a fixed fulcrum with two forces applied to it.

**Ligament** A short band of tough and flexible tissue that connects bones together and stabilises the joint.

**Load** The weight/resistance to be moved. For example, a body part plus anything held or resistance met.

**Load arm** The distance from the fulcrum to the load.

**Longitudinal axis of rotation** An imaginary line passing vertically through the body from top to bottom. A 360 degree turn rotates around this axis.

**Lumen** The internal diameter of a blood vessel.

# M

**Manual guidance** Information given to a performer to help them develop, which involves them being physically manipulated into the correct position.

**Maximum heart rate** The highest achievable heart rate for an individual.

**Mechanical advantage** A second class lever allows a large load to be moved with a relatively small amount of effort.

**Mechanical guidance** Information given to a performer to help them develop that involves apparatus or aids to assist in the learning process.

**Media** A diverse range of technologies that act as a means of mass communication. The media informs, educates and entertains. The media consists of the print media (sometimes referred to as 'the press'), the broadcast media and the internet and social media.

**Mental preparation techniques** A group of techniques, including imagery, mental rehearsal, selective attention and positive thinking, which are performed before performance. They take place within the mind of the performer, without any actual physical movement.

**Minute ventilation** The volume of air inhaled or exhaled from the lungs per minute.

**Motor skill** A learned body movement or action that is created when muscles contract and cause movements at joints.

**Muscular endurance** The ability to move your body and contract your muscles repeatedly without fatigue.

**Muscular strength** The maximum force a muscle or a group of muscles can apply against resistance.

**Musculo-skeletal system** The name given to the combined body system that involves the muscular system and the skeletal system.

# N

**Normative data** Normative data shows the results for 'normal' people. Data is collected from a large sample of people and the most common results are established.

# O

**Open skill** A skill that is affected by the environment and must be adapted to suit the environment. These skills are usually externally paced. For example, a pass within a football game.

**Overload** A greater than normal stress that is applied to the body causing training adaptations to take place.

## goa

The Christian Portuguese had a great deal of influence on the tropical state of Goa, as did the Muslims. The Portuguese use of vinegar and the sour fruits of lokum and tamarind have combined with the Christian preference for pork and a non-vegetarian-Hindu taste for lamb. Seafood, fish and fruits are plentiful. Goans also perfected the vindaloo. Try the pork vindaloo recipe on page 50, or for something milder, the cashew butter chicken on page 47.

## south india

In the south, one finds a Brahmin cuisine, distinctive because strict South Indian Brahmins will not eat tomatoes and beetroot, as they are blood-coloured – nor will they eat garlic or onion. Recipes are based on tamarind, chilli, coconut, yellow lentils and rice. These, combined with a vegetable, make *sambar*, a staple dish eaten with *rasama*, a peppery, lentil-based consommé. These two dishes are the basis of the English-inspired mulligatawny, a staple dish usually eaten twice daily. Meat and seafood are enjoyed by non-vegetarians. Steamed dumplings and pancakes made from fermented ground rice and dhal have spread from Southern India throughout India.

## parsi

Like Christians, the Parsis have no religious dietary restrictions. Their cuisine is not overly hot, so it is a favourite with many foreigners. Traditionally, on Sunday, Parsis (most of whom live in Mumbai) add several dhals to meat, chicken and meatballs (deep fried) with caramelised brown rice.

# spices, mixes and blends

## aadoo mirch spice mix

**ingredients**
4 tablespoons fresh ginger, grated
1 clove garlic, chopped
12 small fresh chillies, chopped
½ teaspoon salt
**Makes 75 g**

1 Grind ginger and garlic in a blender or food processor, or use a mortar and pestle. Remove stalks from chillies and add with salt. Purée to a smooth paste, scrape into a bowl and cover tightly. Will keep for 1 week in the refrigerator.

## masala curry paste

**ingredients**
3 tablespoons fresh ginger, grated
1 teaspoon ground turmeric
1 teaspoon ground cloves
1 teaspoon ground cardamom
2 cloves garlic, crushed
6 tablespoons fresh coriander, chopped
6 tablespoons fresh mint, chopped
½ cup cider vinegar
60 ml peanut oil
2 teaspoons sesame oil
**Makes about 1 cup**

1 Place ginger, turmeric, cloves, cardamom, garlic, coriander, mint and vinegar in a blender or food processor; process until well combined.

2 Heat oils in a frying pan. Add spice mixture. Cook, stirring, until mixture boils, then remove from heat and allow to cool.

## tandoori spice mix

**ingredients**
1 small onion, chopped
3 cloves garlic, crushed
2½ cm fresh ginger, finely chopped
1-2 green chillies, seeded and chopped
1 teaspoon coriander seeds
½ teaspoon cumin seeds
½ teaspoon red chilli powder
1 teaspoon paprika
½ teaspoon salt
**Makes 6 tablespoons**

1 Grind onion, garlic, ginger, chillies and seeds together, using a pestle and mortar, or a coffee grinder kept especially for the purpose. Add chilli powder, paprika and salt and mix well.

## garam masala

**ingredients**
2 teaspoons cardamom seeds
2 teaspoons cumin seeds
2 teaspoons coriander seeds
1 teaspoon black peppercorns
1 teaspoon whole cloves
1 cinnamon stick, broken
½ nutmeg, grated
**Makes 4 tablespoons**

1 Heat a heavy-based frying pan over moderate heat. Add cardamom seeds, cumin seeds, coriander seeds, peppercorns, cloves and cinnamon stick. Cook, stirring, until evenly browned. Allow to cool.

2 Using a mortar and pestle, or a coffee grinder kept especially for the purpose, grind the roasted spices to a fine powder. Add nutmeg and mix well.

# madras curry paste

### ingredients
6 tablespoons ground coriander
4 tablespoons ground cumin
1 tablespoon freshly ground black pepper
1 tablespoon ground turmeric
1 tablespoon black mustard seeds
1 tablespoon chilli powder
4 cloves garlic, crushed
1 tablespoon fresh ginger, finely grated
½ cup vinegar
2 tablespoons oil
**Makes about ¾ cup**

1 Place coriander, cumin, black pepper, turmeric, mustard seeds, chilli powder, garlic, ginger and vinegar in a food processor or blender and process to make a smooth paste. Heat oil in a frying pan over medium heat, add paste and cook, stirring constantly, for 5 minutes or until oil begins to separate from paste.

# vindaloo paste

### ingredients
1 tablespoon coriander seeds
1 teaspoon cumin seeds
1 teaspoon mustard seeds
1 teaspoon ground turmeric
1 teaspoon chilli powder
1½ teaspoons ground ginger
pinch ground fenugreek
1½ teaspoons black pepper, finely ground
1 tablespoon white wine vinegar, plus extra to serve
**Makes about 4 tablespoons**

1 Using a mortar and pestle, or a coffee grinder kept especially for the purpose, grind the whole seeds finely. Add the remaining ground spices.

2 Gradually stir in the vinegar to make a thick, smooth paste. Store in an airtight container and moisten with an additional teaspoon of vinegar just before use.

**Note:** Leftover pastes may be stored in sterile airtight containers in the refrigerator for 8–10 days.

# green masala curry paste

### ingredients
1 teaspoon fenugreek seeds, soaked in cold water overnight
3 cloves garlic, crushed
2 tablespoons fresh ginger, grated
12 tablespoons fresh coriander, chopped
12 tablespoons fresh mint, chopped
½ cup vinegar
1 teaspoon Thai fish sauce
2 teaspoons ground turmeric
1 teaspoon ground cardamom
¼ cup sesame oil
½ cup vegetable oil
**Makes about ¼ cup**

1 Place soaked fenugreek seeds, garlic, ginger, coriander, mint and vinegar in a food processor or blender and process to make a smooth paste. Add fish sauce, turmeric and cardamom and process to combine.

2 Heat the sesame and vegetable oils together in a saucepan over a medium heat for 5 minutes or until hot. Stir in paste and cook, stirring constantly, for 5 minutes or until mixture boils and thickens.

# snacks and entrées

# samosas

## ingredients

250 g plain flour
½ teaspoon salt
30 g butter
4-6 tablespoons water
*filling*
30 g butter
1 onion, finely chopped
2 cloves garlic, crushed
2 green chillies, seeded and chopped
2½ cm fresh ginger, grated
½ teaspoon ground turmeric
½ teaspoon chilli powder
370 g lean minced beef or lamb
1 teaspoon salt
2 teaspoon garam masala
juice of ½ lemon
oil for deep-frying
**makes 30**

1 Sift the flour and salt into a bowl. Rub in the butter, then mix in enough water to form a pliable dough. Knead for 10 minutes, then set aside.

2 To make the filling, melt butter in a frying pan. Add onion, garlic, chillies and ginger and fry for 5–7 minutes until onion is golden.

3 Stir in turmeric and chilli powder, then add the meat and salt. Fry, stirring, until meat is cooked and mixture is fairly dry. Stir in garam masala and lemon juice and cook for 5 minutes more. Remove pan from heat and allow to cool.

4 Divide the dough into 15 balls. Flatten each ball and roll out to a paper-thin circle about 10 cm in diameter. Dampen the edges of each circle with water. Fill each paste with filling, then pinch down the edges to seal securely.

5 Deep-fry the samosas in batches in hot oil for 2–3 minutes or until golden brown. Drain on kitchen towel and serve.

**i**

**preparation time**
25 minutes

**cooking time**
10 minutes

**nutritional value**
fat: 10.3 g
carbohydrate: 6.2 g
protein: 3.5 g

# traditional dhal

### ingredients

180 g brown or red lentils
3½ cups water
1 teaspoon ground turmeric
1 clove garlic, crushed
25 g ghee or clarified butter
1 medium onion, chopped
1 teaspoon garam masala
¼ teaspoon ground ginger
1 teaspoon ground coriander
½ teaspoon cayenne pepper
**serves 4**

1 Wash lentils in cold water. Place lentils, water, turmeric and garlic in a large saucepan and bring to simmering point. Cover and simmer, stirring occasionally, for 30 minutes or until lentils are cooked. Remove cover from pan and bring to the boil to reduce excess liquid.

**preparation time**
3 minutes

**cooking time**
36 minutes

**nutritional value**
fat: 5.9 g
carbohydrate: 18 g
protein: 10.5 g

2 Melt the ghee or butter in a large frying pan, add the onion and cook for 5 minutes or until onion is soft. Stir in garam masala, ginger, coriander and cayenne pepper and cook for 1 minute. Stir spice mixture into lentils and serve immediately.

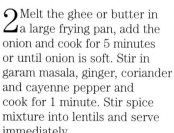

# toor balls

## ingredients

### kofka balls
1 cup toor dhal (toor dhal is also known as toovar dhal)
1 small onion, finely chopped
2 cm fresh ginger, finely chopped
2 cloves garlic, finely chopped
4 green chillies, finely chopped
1 handful coriander leaves, roughly chopped

### curry
4 cups buttermilk or yoghurt
1 teaspoon ground coriander
1 teaspoon cumin
1 teaspoon channa dhal
¼ teaspoon fenugreek
½ teaspoon turmeric
¼ cup desiccated coconut
2½ cm fresh ginger, grated or finely chopped
4 green chillies, finely chopped
salt and freshly ground black pepper to taste

### flavoured oil
2 tablespoons oil
½ teaspoon black mustard seeds
3-4 curry leaves

**serves 4**

1 To make the kofka balls, rinse then soak toor dhal for 2 to 3 hours. Drain and add onion, ginger, garlic and chillies and a large pinch of salt. Grind down to a coarse paste. Cut the larger ingredients into chunks and blend with the dhal using a blender, or mortar and pestle. (Only add a small amount of water, as you do not want this paste to be runny.)

2 Add coriander leaves. Form into flat ball shapes and steam for 20 minutes. Remove from heat and cool.

3 To make the curry, heat buttermilk or yoghurt in a saucepan on medium heat. Add ground coriander, cumin, channa dhal, fenugreek, turmeric and enough desiccated coconut to slightly thicken the sauce. Add ginger and chillies. Season with salt and pepper to taste.

4 Place kofta balls into sauce and gently heat. At the same time, heat a small amount of oil in another pan over a medium heat. Add mustard seeds and curry leaves. When the mustard seeds stop bursting, add oil into the curry and remove from the heat. Place the toor balls on a platter and top with flavoured oil.

**i**

**preparation time**
20 minutes

**cooking time**
25 minutes

**nutritional value**
fat: 28 g
carbohydrate: 32 g
protein: 7 g

# split lentil dhal with ginger and coriander

## ingredients

200 g dried split red lentils
3½ cups water
½ teaspoon turmeric
1 tablespoon vegetable oil
1 cm fresh ginger, finely chopped
1 teaspoon cumin seeds
1 teaspoon ground coriander
salt and freshly ground black pepper
4 tablespoons fresh coriander, chopped, plus extra leaves to garnish
½ teaspoon paprika

**serves 4**

*i*

**preparation time**
5 minutes

**cooking time**
40 minutes

**nutritional value**
fat: 5.6 g
carbohydrate: 19 g
protein: 12.1 g

**1** Rinse the lentils and drain well, then place in a large saucepan with the water. Bring to the boil, skimming off any sediment, then stir in the turmeric. Reduce the heat and partly cover pan. Simmer for 30–35 minutes, until thickened, stirring occasionally.

**2** Heat the oil in a small frying pan, then add ginger and cumin seeds and fry for 30 seconds or until cumin seeds start to pop. Stir in ground coriander and fry for 1 minute.

**3** Season lentils with plenty of salt and pepper, then add toasted spices. Stir in the chopped coriander, mixing well. Transfer to a serving dish and garnish with paprika and coriander leaves.

# crunchy split peas

### ingredients

85 g yellow split peas
85 g green split peas
2 teaspoons bicarbonate of soda
oil for deep-frying
½ teaspoon chilli powder
½ teaspoon ground coriander
pinch of ground cinnamon
pinch of ground cloves
1 teaspoon salt
**serves 4**

1 Place the split peas in a large bowl, cover with water, stir in bicarbonate of soda and set aside to soak overnight.

2 Rinse the peas under cold running water and drain thoroughly. Set aside for at least 30 minutes, then spread out on kitchen towel to dry. Heat about 5 cm of oil in a frying pan and cook split peas in batches until golden.

3 Using a slotted spoon, remove the peas and drain on kitchen towel. Transfer cooked peas to a dish, sprinkle with chilli powder, coriander, cinnamon, cloves and salt and toss to coat.

4 Allow peas to cool and store in an airtight container.

**i**

**preparation time**
1 hour, plus
11 hours soaking

**cooking time**
20 minutes

**nutritional value**
fat: 30 g
carbohydrate: 20 g
protein: 10 g

# soups
# and
# salads

# mulligatawny soup

## ingredients

1 tablespoon vegetable oil
2 onions, chopped
1 green apple, cored, peeled and
    chopped
1 clove garlic, crushed
2 tablespoons lemon juice
1 tablespoon curry powder
1 teaspoon brown sugar
½ teaspoon ground cumin
¼ teaspoon ground coriander
2 tablespoons plain flour
8 cups chicken stock
2 medium skinless chicken breast
    fillets, cut into small cubes
⅓ cup rice
freshly ground black pepper
chilli sauce to serve

**serves 4**

**preparation time**
15 minutes

**cooking time**
30 minutes

**nutritional value**
fat: 14 g
carbohydrate: 29 g
protein: 35 g

1 Heat the oil in a large saucepan over medium heat. Add onions, apple and garlic and cook, stirring, for 5 minutes or until onions have softened. Add lemon juice, curry powder, sugar, cumin and coriander and cook over low heat, stirring, for 10 minutes or until fragrant.

2 Blend flour with a little stock and stir into curry mixture. Add chicken, rice and remaining stock to pan, and bring to the boil, stirring constantly. Reduce heat, cover and simmer for 20 minutes or until the chicken and rice are cooked. Season to taste with black pepper. When serving, top each bowl with a dash of chilli sauce.

# lentil soup

### ingredients

1 tablespoon ghee or vegetable oil
175 g red lentils
1 teaspoon mustard seeds
½ teaspoon ground coriander
1 teaspoon ground cumin
1 teaspoon turmeric
1 cinnamon stick
5 cloves garlic, finely chopped
2 cm fresh ginger, finely chopped
7 fresh curry leaves, bruised and tied
   together
1 medium onion, finely chopped
1 medium green chilli, whole but split
4 cups rich vegetable stock
1 tomatoes, finely diced
½ small eggplant, finely diced
1 small carrot, finely diced
1 medium potato, peeled and diced
juice of 4 lemons
salt
fresh coriander, to garnish
4 tablespoons yoghurt, to garnish
**serves 4**

1 In a large saucepan, heat the ghee and add lentils, mustard seeds, coriander, cumin, turmeric, cinnamon stick, garlic, ginger, curry leaves, onion and green chilli. Cook over low heat for 5 minutes until spices are aromatic and deep brown in colour and the onion has softened.

**i**

**preparation time**
20 minutes

**cooking time**
1 hour 10 minutes

**nutritional value**
fat: 7 g
carbohydrate: 16 g
protein: 28 g

2 Add the vegetable stock and simmer until lentils are soft: about 30–45 minutes.

3 Remove cinnamon stick, whole green chilli and curry leaves.

4 Blend with a hand-held mixer or food processor until smooth, then return the soup to the saucepan.

5 Add diced vegetables and simmer for a further 20 minutes or until vegetables are soft.

6 Add lemon juice, salt to taste and chopped coriander. Stir well and serve with a dollop of yoghurt. Garnish with a few extra coriander leaves.

# coconut rice salad

## ingredients

350 g long grain rice
60 g ghee
100 g coconut threads
100 g cashews
1 teaspoon yellow mustard seeds
5 dried curry leaves
2 teaspoons lentils
1 large onion, finely chopped
3 cloves garlic, minced
1 teaspoon turmeric
½ teaspoon chilli powder
½ teaspoon salt
225 ml coconut milk
600 ml water

**serves 4**

**preparation time**
1 hour 10 minutes

**cooking time**
20 minutes

**nutritional value**
fat: 21.5 g
carbohydrate: 55 g
protein: 19.5 g

**1** Rinse the rice under cold water. Soak in cold water for 1 hour. Drain well. Meanwhile, heat 1 tablespoon of the ghee in a saucepan, add the coconut and cashews and toast until golden. Set aside.

**2** Heat the remaining ghee in the same pan. Add the mustard seeds, curry leaves and lentils. Stir and cook until fragrant. Add the onion and garlic and continue cooking until the onion has softened.

**3** Add the turmeric, chilli, a pinch of salt and coconut milk and simmer for 5 minutes. Add the rice and water. Cover and simmer until the rice is tender. Lift the lid and stir gently then cool.

**4** Add half the coconut and cashews and stir through to distribute the garnish with the remaining coconut and cashew mixture. Serve immediately.

# lamb salad with black onion seeds and sesame

## ingredients

### marinade
1 large onion, chopped
2 cm piece fresh ginger, grated
juice of 1 lemon
1 tablespoon water
½ cup plain yoghurt
2 teaspoons ground coriander
2 teaspoons ground cumin
½ teaspoon ground turmeric
¼ teaspoon cayenne pepper
1 tablespoon garam masala
¼ teaspoon mace
1 teaspoon salt

### salad
12 large lamb cutlets
1 cup sesame seeds
½ cup black onion seeds, also called
  nigella (available from Indian
  grocery stores)
250 g baby spinach leaves
200 g mixed baby lettuce leaves
4 spring onions, sliced
40 ml white vinegar
60 ml peanut oil
few drops toasted sesame oil
salt and freshly ground black pepper
**serves 4**

1 Place the marinade ingredients in a food processor and process until the mixture is smooth.

2 Pour mixture over the lamb cutlets, coating both sides of the lamb. Marinate for 2 hours. Preheat the oven to 220°C. Mix the sesame seeds and onion seeds together and place them on a plate. If black onion seeds are unavailable, simply use extra sesame seeds.

3 Remove the lamb cutlets from the marinade one at a time. Dip each cutlet in the sesame mixture, coating both sides. Place the coated cutlets on a non-stick baking tray and bake in the preheated oven for 10 minutes until medium rare.

4 Meanwhile, mix the salad leaves with the spring onions in a large salad bowl. Whisk together the vinegar, oil and sesame oil with salt and pepper to taste, continuing to whisk until the dressing is thick. Toss the salad with the dressing. Arrange 2 cutlets on each plate and serve immediately.

*i*

**preparation time**
2 hours 15 minutes

**cooking time**
10 minutes

**nutritional value**
fat: 22 g
carbohydrate: 10 g
protein: 11 g

# bread
# and rice

# spiced rice

## ingredients

1½ cups basmati rice
4 cups water
½ teaspoon salt
2 tablespoons lemon juice
2 tablespoons ghee
1 medium red onion, chopped
3 tablespoons cashews
3 tablespoons sultanas
¼ teaspoon fennel seeds
¼ teaspoon cumin seeds
¼ teaspoon white mustard seeds
¼ teaspoon ground turmeric
1 teaspoon ghee, extra

**serves 4**

*i*

**preparation time**
5 minutes

**cooking time**
25 minutes

**nutritional value**
fat: 14.5 g
carbohydrate: 72 g
protein: 7 g

**1** Rinse the rice well in a sieve under running water. Bring the water to the boil, and add salt and lemon juice. Stir in the rice and, when water returns to the boil, turn down heat and simmer for 18 minutes, until rice is just tender. Drain and rinse with hot water. Set aside.

**2** Heat the ghee in a large frying pan. Add the onion and cook until transparent. Add cashews and sultanas and cook briefly. Add spices and the extra teaspoon of ghee and cook, stirring constantly, for 2 minutes.

**3** Add the drained rice, gently toss to combine ingredients and reheat the rice. Serve hot with curries or grilled meats.

# simple pilau rice

## ingredients

400 g basmati rice
6 cloves
1 cinnamon stick, crushed
6 green cardamom pods, crushed
½ teaspoon ground turmeric
55 g raisins
30 g slivered almonds
2 bay leaves
1 tablespoon sugar
salt
7 tablespoons ghee or oil
½ teaspoon cumin seeds
1 tablespoon fresh ginger, grated
**serves 4-6**

**preparation time**
30 minutes

**cooking time**
18 minutes

**nutritional value**
fat: 28 g
carbohydrate: 75 g
protein: 6.7 g

1 Rinse the rice well in a sieve under running water, then soak in cold water for 10 minutes. Drain and spread on a clean cloth to dry.

2 Transfer the rice to a platter. Sprinkle over the cloves, some of the cinnamon, the cardamom pods, turmeric, raisins, almonds, bay leaves, sugar and salt.

3 Drizzle over half a teaspoon of melted ghee or oil. Using your hand, mix the spices thoroughly into the rice. Leave for 15 minutes.

4 Heat the remaining ghee or oil in a large saucepan. Add cumin seeds, ginger and rice mixture. Fry gently for 5 minutes until rice is transparent.

5 Add hot water, covering rice by 1 cm. Bring to the boil, reduce heat and simmer until all liquid is absorbed and rice is tender. Before serving, turn rice over gently.

**2** Knead the dough on a lightly floured work surface for 5–10 minutes, then place in a bowl, cover with a cloth and leave to rest for 30–60 minutes.

**3** Knead the dough for 2–3 minutes. Divide into 6 balls of equal size, then flatten each ball into a circle about 12½ cm in diameter.

**4** Heat an ungreased griddle or electric frying pan until hot. Place one chapati at a time on the hot surface. As soon as bubbles appear on the surface of the chapati, turn it over. Press down on chapati with a thick cloth so that it cooks evenly.

**5** To finish chapati, place under a hot grill until it puffs up slightly, being careful not to burn.

**6** Repeat with the remaining dough circles. Keep cooked chapatis hot in a covered, napkin-lined basket.

# chapatis

### ingredients

250 g wholemeal flour
1 teaspoon salt
1 cup water
**makes 15**

**1** Sift the flour and salt into a bowl. Make a well in the centre and add water, a little at a time, using your fingers to incorporate the surrounding flour to make a smooth, pliable dough.

**i**

**preparation time**
1 hour 10 minutes

**cooking time**
30 minutes

**nutritional value**
fat: 0.5 g
carbohydrate: 10 g
protein: 2 g

# fresh corn bread

## ingredients

250 g fresh corn kernels
½ teaspoon salt
2 tablespoons fresh coriander, finely chopped
145 g plain flour, plus extra for dusting
1-2 tablespoons ghee
**serves 4**

**1** In a blender or food processor, blend corn and salt until finely puréed.

**2** Transfer mixture to a mixing bowl and add coriander. Add flour, a little at a time, until mixture is kneadable (it should be a little tacky).

**3** Divide the dough into 12 pieces, then roll each piece out into a circle about 15 cm in diameter. If dough circles are tacky, use some extra flour to absorb the moisture. Once rolled, brush each circle with a little melted ghee.

**4** Heat a griddle or frying pan and add a little ghee. Add one piece of dough and cook until underside is spotted with brown. Turn over and cook other side. Remove cooked bread and keep warm in foil while cooking the other breads.

**preparation time**
12 minutes

**cooking time**
45 minutes

**nutritional value**
fat: 7 g
carbohydrate: 32 g
protein: 7.5 g

# potato naan

## ingredients

*dough*
1 cup plain full-fat yoghurt
1½ cups boiling water
2 cups plain flour
3 cups stoneground wholemeal flour
1 tablespoon yeast
2 teaspoons salt
1 teaspoon sugar
2 tablespoons peanut oil
1 egg, beaten
3 tablespoons black sesame seeds

*filling*
500 g potatoes, peeled
1 onion, finely diced
4 mint leaves, finely sliced
¼ cup parsley, chopped
½ cup coriander leaves, chopped
¼ teaspoon cumin
¼ teaspoon turmeric
salt and pepper

**serves 4**

**1** Preheat the oven to 200°C. Mix the yoghurt with boiling water and stir well. Set aside for 5 minutes.

**2** Mix plain flour with 1 cup of wholemeal flour and add the yeast. Add yoghurt mixture and stir with a wooden spoon for 3 minutes, then allow to rest for 30 minutes.

**3** Add salt, sugar, oil and black sesame seeds and enough of the remaining flour to form a firm but moist dough.

**4** Knead on a floured work surface until dough is very silky and elastic. Allow dough to rest in an oiled bowl for 1 hour or until doubled in size.

**5** To make the potato filling, boil the potatoes in water until soft. Mix hot potato with onion, mint leaves, parsley, coriander, cumin, turmeric and salt and pepper and mash until soft but not sloppy. Allow to cool.

**6** Punch down the dough and divide into 12 equal pieces. Roll each piece into a circle about 15 cm in diameter. Place a large tablespoon of filling in the centre of each circle, and lift both edges to seal. Pinch the seam together very well. Allow to rise for 10 minutes, then brush with beaten egg and sprinkle with sesame seeds. Bake for 15–20 minutes or until golden and crisp.

**i**

**preparation time**
2 hours 25 minutes

**cooking time**
20 minutes

**nutritional value**
fat: 16 g
carbohydrate: 14 g
protein: 28.5 g

# side
# dishes

# green bean salad with coriander and ginger

### ingredients

700 g snake beans
2 cm fresh ginger
1 tablespoon vegetable oil
1 tablespoon sesame oil
1 teaspoon mustard seeds
2 teaspoons cumin
½ teaspoon turmeric
1 green chilli, finely chopped
145 ml chicken or vegetable stock
juice of 2 lemons
1 bunch coriander, washed, dried and
    chopped
salt
85 g peanuts, roasted and chopped
lemon wedges

**serves 4**

**i**

**preparation time**
8 minutes

**cooking time**
18 minutes

**nutritional value**
fat: 20 g
carbohydrate: 6 g
protein: 11.5 g

1 Trim the beans to lengths of 8 cm and discard any discoloured ends. Peel the ginger and cut into fine matchstick-sized pieces.

2 In a wok, heat the vegetable and sesame oils and when hot, add the mustard seeds. Allow to cook for a moment or two, until the seeds start popping. Add the ginger and cook for a further minute. Add cumin, turmeric and chilli and stir until fragrant: about 2 minutes.

3 Add the beans and toss in flavoured oil to coat thoroughly. Add the stock and simmer for 5–8 minutes or until the liquid has almost completely evaporated, and beans are tender.

4 Add lemon juice, coriander and salt. Stir thoroughly to combine all ingredients, then let cool. Serve garnished with roasted, chopped peanuts and lemon wedges if desired.

# chickpea salad with spinach

## ingredients

1 cup dried chickpeas
1 medium onion, peeled and cut in half
2 small onions, peeled and diced
½ teaspoon cloves, diced
2 bay leaves
30 ml peanut or olive oil
2 cloves garlic, chopped
½ teaspoon turmeric
1 teaspoon cumin
1 teaspoon garam masala
1 ½ tablespoons tomato paste
1 red capsicum, sliced
2 medium zucchinis, sliced on the diagonal
salt and pepper
500 g spinach

**serves 4**

**1** Pick over the chickpeas and remove any that are discoloured. Place all remaining chickpeas in a large saucepan and cover with cold water. Place onion halves in saucepan with the chickpeas, add the cloves and bay leaves and bring to boil. Simmer for

10 minutes. Remove from heat, cover and allow to steep for 2 hours. Then strain the chickpeas, keeping the water.

**2** Heat the oil and cook the diced onions and garlic. Add all the spices and cook them briefly to release fragrance. Add the chickpeas and 2 cups of the soaking water, tomato paste and the capsicum.

**3** Cover and simmer gently for about 20 minutes until chickpeas soften and liquid evaporates. Add the zucchini and salt and pepper, and stir well. Remove from heat, allow to cool slightly, then fold through the spinach leaves. Cool completely and serve.

**i**

**preparation time**
2 hours 10 minutes

**cooking time**
30 minutes

**nutritional value**
fat: 10 g
carbohydrate: 24 g
protein: 12 g

# cauliflower and peas in chilli sauce

## ingredients

2 tablespoons oil
1 teaspoon mustard seeds
½ teaspoon chilli powder
pinch of asafoetida
1 cauliflower, divided into florets
125 g fresh or frozen peas (thawed if frozen)
1 potato, cut into 1 cm cubes
2 tomatoes, peeled and finely chopped
½ teaspoon turmeric
½ teaspoon aadoo mirch spice mix (see page 6)
pinch of salt
1 tablespoon coriander leaves, chopped
1 teaspoon molasses
400 ml water

**serves 4**

**i**

**preparation time**
10 minutes

**cooking time**
35 minutes

**nutritional value**
fat: 9.5 g
carbohydrate: 13 g
protein: 6.5 g

**1** Heat the oil in a heavy-based saucepan over moderately high heat and add mustard seeds. As soon as the seeds pop, stir in chilli powder and asafoetida. Shake the pan briefly over heat, then add the cauliflower florets and peas.

**2** Fry, stirring, for a few seconds, then add potato cubes, tomatoes, turmeric, aadoo mirch, salt, coriander and molasses.

**3** Stir well, cover and cook for 3–4 minutes, then add the water, mixing thoroughly. Reduce heat, cover and simmer for about 30 minutes or until vegetables are tender and sauce has thickened slightly. Serve hot with chapatis (see page 26).

# mogul salad

### ingredients

175 g mung bean sprouts
2 cucumbers, diced
3 teaspoons grated fresh or desiccated
  coconut
2 small tomatoes, diced
4 tablespoons coriander leaves,
  chopped
½ bunch mint leaves, chopped
½ bunch basil leaves, chopped
1 bunch spring onions, chopped
2 tablespoons lemon juice
salt and freshly ground black pepper
**serves 4**

1 Place bean sprouts, cucumbers, coconut, tomatoes, coriander, mint and basil leaves, spring onions, lemon juice and salt and black pepper in a bowl and toss to combine. Cover and stand at room temperature for 2 hours before serving.

**i**

**preparation time**
10 minutes, plus
2 hours standing

**nutritional value**
fat: 1 g
carbohydrate: 9 g
protein: 4.5 g

# vegetable korma

## ingredients

2 tablespoons vegetable oil
2 tablespoons green masala curry paste
1 teaspoon chilli powder
1 tablespoon fresh ginger, finely grated
2 cloves garlic, crushed
1 onion, chopped
500 g cauliflower, cut into florets
200 g green beans, cut in half
3 baby eggplants, cubed
2 carrots, sliced
125 g button mushrooms
400 g canned tomatoes, mashed in their juices
1 cup vegetable stock

**serves 4**

**i**

**preparation time**
10 minutes

**cooking time**
30 minutes

**nutritional value**
fat: 14 g
carbohydrate: 11 g
protein: 8 g

1 Heat the oil in a saucepan over medium heat, stir in masala paste and chilli powder and cook for 2 minutes. Add the ginger, garlic and onion and cook, stirring, for 3 minutes or until onion is soft. Add the cauliflower, beans, eggplants, carrots and mushrooms and cook, stirring, for 5 minutes.

2 Stir in the tomatoes and stock, and bring to the boil. Reduce heat and simmer stirring occasionally, for 20 minutes or until vegetables are tender.

# potato and pea bhajis

### ingredients

3-4 tablespoons oil
1 onion, thinly sliced
1 teaspoon turmeric
1 teaspoon cumin seeds
¼ teaspoon ground ginger
1 green chilli, seeded and chopped
500 g potatoes, peeled and diced
250 g fresh or frozen peas (thawed if
   frozen)
fresh coriander leaves, to garnish
**serves 4**

1 Heat the oil in a flameproof casserole dish, add the onion and fry for 5–7 minutes, stirring frequently, until browned but not crisp.

2 Stir in turmeric, cumin seeds, ginger and chilli, then add potatoes and cook gently for 5 minutes, stirring frequently.

3 Stir in the peas. Cover casserole and simmer over very low heat for 15–20 minutes, or until potatoes are tender but retain their shape. Garnish with coriander and serve.

**i**

**preparation time**
8 minutes

**cooking time**
30 minutes

**nutritional value**
fat: 16 g
carbohydrate: 24 g
protein: 7 g

# poultry
# and
# meat

# tandoori chicken

## ingredients

2 x 1 kg fresh chickens
3 tablespoons tandoori spice mix
  (see page 6)
200 g natural yoghurt
2 tablespoons lemon juice
1 tablespoon butter, melted
lettuce leaves, onion rings, tomato
  wedges and lemon

**serves 4-6**

1 Rinse chickens inside and out and pat dry with kitchen towel. Make deep gashes in thighs and on each side of breast.

**i**

**preparation time**
12 hours
10 minutes

**cooking time**
20 minutes

**nutritional value**
fat: 36.5 g
carbohydrate: 3 g
protein: 54 g

2 Mix tandoori spice mix, yoghurt, lemon juice and melted butter together. Place chickens in a stainless steel or non-metalic dish and spread mixture over, rubbing well into gashes. Cover and refrigerate for 12 hours.

3 Preheat the oven to 190°C. Place chickens on a roasting rack in a baking dish and spoon remaining marinade over them.

4 Roast for 1 hour, baste with pan juices during cooking. When cooked, cover with foil and rest for 10 minutes before serving.

5 Arrange crisp lettuce leaves on a large platter and cover with onion rings. Cut chicken into portions and place on the platter. Garnish with tomato wedges and lemon slices and serve immediately.

# roasted patiala chicken breasts

### ingredients

2 tablespoons natural yoghurt
4 skinless chicken breasts
1 teaspoon salt
4 cloves garlic, chopped
2 tablespoons coriander leaves, chopped, plus extra leaves to garnish
½ teaspoon turmeric
4 cardamom pods, husks discarded
½ cup butter, melted
2 tablespoons tandoori spice mix (see page 6)
1 medium onion, peeled and pureed
**serves 4**

**i**

**preparation time**
2 hours 15 minutes

**cooking time**
25 minutes

**nutritional value**
fat: 27 g
carbohydrate: 25 g
protein: 80 g

**1** Cook the onion in a small saucepan over a medium heat for 5 minutes and cool.

**2** Using a mortar and pestle grind the salt, garlic, coriander and cardamom seeds to a paste. Transfer to a non-metallic bowl, stir in the yoghurt, butter, tandoori paste and onion puree, mix together well.

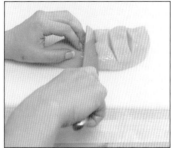

**3** Score each chicken breast 4 times with a sharp knife, and coat chicken thoroughly. Cover and chill for 6 hours.

**4** Preheat the oven to 220°C. Place the chicken breasts on a rack in a roasting dish and cook for 20–25 minutes until tender and the juices run clear when the chicken is pierced with a skewer. Serve with basmati rice.

# kashmiri chicken

### ingredients

1 onion, finely chopped
3 tablespoons fresh ginger, grated
2 cloves garlic, crushed
½ teaspoon ground coriander
1½ teaspoons anchovy essence
1 cup ground almonds or cashews
1 tablespoon oil
4 chicken pieces, skinned
1 cup chicken stock
1 cup thick coconut milk
2 teaspoons light brown sugar

**serves 4**

**i**

**preparation time**
10 minutes

**cooking time**
1 hour

**nutritional value**
fat: 50 g
carbohydrate: 7 g
protein: 80.5 g

**1** Mix onion, ginger, garlic, coriander and anchovy essence with ground almonds or cashews to form a paste.

**2** Heat the oil in a large heavy-based saucepan. Add the paste and stir over moderate heat for 5 minutes.

**3** Add the chicken pieces and cook for 15 minutes, stirring frequently to coat in the spice mixture and seal.

**4** Pour in the stock, stirring to combine with the spice mixture. Bring to the boil, reduce heat and simmer for 20 minutes.

**5** Stir in the coconut milk and brown sugar, turn heat to lowest setting and simmer for 20 minutes more.

# northern indian chicken curry

### ingredients

4 tablespoons ghee
2 cups sliced onions
2 teaspoons salt
1 teaspoon freshly ground black pepper
2 teaspoons sugar
1 tablespoon garlic, minced
1 tablespoon ginger, minced
2 tablespoons red chili, minced
1 bay leaf
2 tablespoons garam masala (see page 6)
8 large chicken drumsticks
2 cups diced tomatoes
1 tablespoon tomato paste

**serves 4**

**i**

**preparation time**
10 minutes

**cooking time**
1 hour

**nutritional value**
fat: 42 g
carbohydrate: 11 g
protein: 92 g

1 In a large saucepan, heat the ghee. Stir-fry the onions until glossy. Season with salt, black pepper and sugar. Continue to stir-fry until soft but do not allow to brown.

2 Add the garlic, ginger, chilli, bay leaf and garam masala. Stir-fry for 1 to 2 minutes until spices become aromatic.

3 Add the chicken pieces, tomatoes and tomato paste and cook over a medium heat for about 20 minutes, adding water a little at a time if needed. Taste and adjust seasoning with salt, pepper, and sugar. Serve with Indian naan bread.

# salad of spiced chicken and dhal

### ingredients

6 cups vegetable stock
1½ cups dried lentils
juice of 2 lemons
40 ml vegetable oil
1 tablespoon madras curry paste
  (see page 7)
1 tablespoon garam masala
1 teaspoon turmeric
salt and pepper
4 large skinless chicken breast fillets
1½ cups vegetable stock, extra
1 small cauliflower, cut into florets
1½ cups fresh or frozen peas
2 small tomatoes, seeded and diced
1 cucumber, peeled and diced
2 spring onions, sliced
2 tablespoons fresh mint, chopped
2 large bunches watercress, trimmed
fresh mint, to garnish
spring onion, to garnish
**serves 4**

1 Bring the vegetable stock to the boil and add the lentils. Simmer until lentils are tender: about 20 minutes. Drain well, then transfer lentils to a large bowl and add lemon juice and 1 tablespoon of oil. Mix well, cover and chill.

**i**

**preparation time**
15 minutes

**cooking time**
20 minutes

**nutritional value**
fat: 36 g
carbohydrate: 41 g
protein: 110 g

2 Combine the curry paste, garam masala and turmeric in a plastic bag with salt and pepper to taste, then add chicken. Seal bag and shake vigorously. Heat a grill pan or nonstick frying pan with the remaining oil until smoking. Add chicken to the pan and fry on both sides until golden brown and cooked through: about 5 minutes. Remove the chicken and set aside.

3 To the used pan, add the extra stock and bring to a boil. Add cauliflower and peas and cook over high heat until vegetables are tender-crisp and most of the liquid has evaporated: about 5 minutes. Add the vegetable mixture to the lentils and mix well. Add the tomatoes, cucumber, spring onions and fresh mint and mix well, adding salt and pepper to taste.

4 Slice chicken into diagonal strips then gently mix into salad. Arrange watercress on a platter and top with salad mixture, arranging so that plenty of chicken is visible. Garnish with fresh mint and spring onion.

# chicken biryani with rice pilau

### ingredients

3 tablespoons ghee
3 onions, sliced
1½ kg chicken pieces
2 teaspoons fresh ginger, grated
3 cloves garlic, crushed
½ teaspoon ground cumin
½ teaspoon ground cinnamon
¼ teaspoon ground cloves
¼ teaspoon ground cardamom
¼ teaspoon ground nutmeg
½ teaspoon flour
1 cup chicken stock
½ cup natural yoghurt
½ cup cream
¼ cup cashews, chopped

*rice pilau*
2 tablespoons ghee
½ teaspoon ground saffron
½ teaspoon ground cardamom
1 teaspoon salt
200 g basmati rice, well washed
4 cups chicken stock
2 tablespoons sultanas
**serves 4**

**i**

**preparation time**
20 minutes

**cooking time**
1 hour 30 minutes

**nutritional value**
fat: 59 g
carbohydrate: 54 g
protein: 90.5 g

1 Heat ghee in a large frying pan and cook onions for 2–3 minutes or until golden brown. Remove from pan and set aside.

2 Add the chicken to the pan and cook until well browned on all sides. Remove from pan and set aside.

3 Combine ginger, garlic, cumin, cinnamon, cloves, cardamom, nutmeg and flour. Stir into pan and cook for 1–2 minutes. Add stock, yoghurt and cream, and stir to lift pan sediment.

4 Return the chicken to the pan, with half the onions. Cover and simmer for 15–20 minutes. Remove from heat and let stand, covered, for 15 minutes. Preheat the oven to 180°C.

5 To make the rice pilau, heat the ghee in a large saucepan. Cook spices, salt and rice for 1–2 minutes. Pour in stock and bring to boil. Add sultanas, reduce heat and cook gently for 10–15 minutes, until most of the stock is absorbed. Cover and set aside for 10 minutes.

6 Transfer half the rice to a large ovenproof dish, top with chicken pieces, then with remaining rice. Drizzle over the sauce from the chicken, and top with remaining onions and cashews. Cover and bake for 20–30 minutes.

# cashew butter chicken

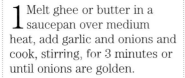

### ingredients

40 g ghee or butter
2 cloves garlic, crushed
2 small onions, finely chopped
1 tablespoon madras curry paste
  (see page 7)
1 tablespoon ground coriander
½ teaspoon ground nutmeg
550 g chicken thigh or breast fillets,
  cut into 2 cm cubes
40 g cashews, roasted and ground
1 cup double cream
2 tablespoons coconut milk
**serves 4**

**i**

**preparation time**
10 minutes

**cooking time**
1 hour

**nutritional value**
fat: 50 g
carbohydrate: 6 g
protein: 30 g

1 Melt ghee or butter in a saucepan over medium heat, add garlic and onions and cook, stirring, for 3 minutes or until onions are golden.

2 Stir in curry paste, coriander and nutmeg and cook for 2 minutes or until fragrant.

3 Add chicken and cook, stirring, for 5 minutes or until chicken is brown.

4 Add cashews, cream and coconut milk, bring to a boil, reduce heat and simmer, stirring occasionally, for 40 minutes or until chicken is tender.

# masala duck curry

### ingredients

1 tablespoon sesame oil
2 kg duck, cleaned and cut into 8 pieces
1 onion, chopped
2 small fresh red chillies, finely chopped
1 stalk lemongrass, finely chopped or ½ teaspoon dried lemongrass, soaked in hot water until soft
2 tablespoons green masala curry paste (see page 7)
1½ cups coconut milk
3 fresh or dried curry leaves
1 tablespoon lime juice
1 tablespoon brown sugar
1 tablespoon coriander leaves, chopped
30 g basil leaves
3 fresh green chillies, seeded and sliced
2 fresh red chillies, seeded and sliced

**serves 4**

i

**preparation time**
20 minutes

**cooking time**
1 hour 10 minutes

**nutritional value**
fat: 10.2 g
carbohydrate: 9 g
protein: 60 g

1 Heat the oil in a deep frying pan over medium heat. Add the duck and cook, turning frequently, for 10 minutes or until brown on all sides. Remove and drain on kitchen towel.

2 Add the onion, chopped red chillies and lemongrass to pan and cook, stirring, for 3 minutes or until onion is golden. Stir in masala paste and cook for 2 minutes longer or until fragrant.

3 Stir in the coconut milk, curry leaves, lime juice and sugar and return duck to pan. Bring to boil and simmer, stirring occasionally, for 45 minutes.

4 Add coriander, basil and sliced green and red chillies and cook for 10 minutes longer, or until duck is tender.

# mustard chilli pork

## ingredients

750 g pork fillets
55 g butter, melted
30 g ghee
2 tablespoons peanut oil
3 onions, chopped
1 tablespoon black mustard seeds
2 cloves garlic, crushed
2 red chillies, chopped
½ teaspoon ground cumin
½ teaspoon ground turmeric
1 tablespoon brown sugar
1 cup water
1 tablespoon lime juice
8 lime leaves
**serves 4**

1 Preheat the oven to 180°C. Trim the meat of all visible fat, brush with melted butter and bake in an ovenproof dish for 30 minutes.

**preparation time**
5 minutes

**cooking time**
30 minutes

**nutritional value**
fat: 33 g
carbohydrate: 8 g
protein: 42.5 g

2 Meanwhile, heat the ghee and oil in a saucepan, and cook the onions, mustard seeds, garlic and chillies for 2–3 minutes or until onions are soft.

3 Stir in cumin, turmeric, brown sugar, water, lime juice and lime leaves. Bring to the boil, then reduce heat and simmer, uncovered, for 10 minutes or until mixture reduces and thickens.

4 Transfer mixture to a food processor or blender. Process until smooth, then return to pan. Slice the pork diagonally and add to mustard mixture. Heat through gently and serve.

# pork vindaloo

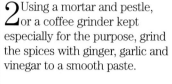

## ingredients

3 small dried red chillies
1 teaspoon cumin seeds
1½ teaspoons coriander seeds
2 cloves
4-6 black peppercorns
2½ cm cinnamon stick
2½ cm fresh ginger, grated
2 cloves garlic, chopped
3 tablespoons white vinegar
500 g lean pork, cut in 2 cm cubes
pinch of salt
water
3 tablespoons oil
2 onions, finely chopped
red chillies, to garnish
**serves 4**

1 Dry-fry the chillies, cumin seeds, coriander seeds, cloves, peppercorns and the cinnamon stick in a frying pan for a few minutes, until the mixture starts to crackle. Do not let it burn.

**i**

**preparation time**
10 minutes

**cooking time**
50 minutes

**nutritional value**
fat: 16.5 g
carbohydrate: 3 g
protein: 28 g

2 Using a mortar and pestle, or a coffee grinder kept especially for the purpose, grind the spices with ginger, garlic and vinegar to a smooth paste.

3 Place the pork in a saucepan with salt. Pour in enough water to cover meat by about 2½ cm. Bring to the boil, reduce heat and simmer for 45 minutes or until meat is tender.

4 Meanwhile, heat the oil in a large frying pan. Fry the onions for about 10 minutes, until golden. Stir in the spice paste and fry for 2 minutes more, stirring constantly.

5 Drain the meat, reserving the cooking liquid, and add it to the pan. Stir well, cover and cook for 10 minutes over moderate heat.

6 Add about 2 cups of reserved cooking liquid. Stir well, cover and cook for 15–20 minutes more, or until meat is coated in a thick spicy sauce.

7 Serve at once, garnished with red chillies, or tip into a casserole dish, cool, and refrigerate for reheating next day.

# lamb korma

## ingredients

1½ kg shoulder of lamb
salt and freshly ground black pepper
2 tablespoons ghee
1 red onion, finely chopped
1 clove garlic, finely chopped
1 tablespoon green masala curry paste
  (see page 7)
¼ teaspoon ground ginger
¼ teaspoon turmeric
⅛ teaspoon cayenne pepper
2 tablespoons flour
1¼ cups chicken stock
¾ cup sultanas
145 ml yoghurt
1 tablespoon lemon juice
**serves 4**

**i**

**preparation time**
10 minutes

**cooking time**
1 hour 15 minutes

**nutritional value**
fat: 27 g
carbohydrate: 26 g
protein: 64 g

**1** Cut the lamb from the bone and chop into 4 cm cubes. Season with salt and pepper.

**2** Heat the ghee in a large, heavy-based saucepan, add one third of the lamb and brown well on all sides. Remove and brown the remainder in 2 batches.

**3** Add onion and garlic and fry until transparent. Stir in curry paste, spices and flour and cook for 1 minute. Add chicken stock, sultanas and lamb. Bring to the boil, cover and simmer gently for

1 hour or until lamb is very tender. Stir occasionally during cooking.

**4** Stir in yoghurt and lemon juice.

# tandoori lamb cutlets

## ingredients

8 lamb cutlets
*marinade*
4 tablespoons natural yoghurt
1 teaspoon fresh ginger, grated
1 clove garlic, crushed
1 tablespoon lime juice
1 teaspoon cumin
¼ teaspoon ground cardamom
¼ teaspoon chilli powder
¼ teaspoon garam masala
**serves 4**

*i*

**preparation time**
40 minutes

**cooking time**
8 minutes

**nutritional value**
fat: 40 g
carbohydrate: 1 g
protein: 20 g

1 Trim meat of all visible fat and set aside.

2 To make the marinade, combine the yoghurt, ginger, garlic, lime juice, cumin, cardamom, chilli powder and garam masala. Add cutlets, toss to coat and set aside to marinate for 30 minutes.

3 Remove cutlets from marinade. Grill or barbecue for 6–8 minutes, turning and basting with marinade frequently.

# lamb and spinach curry

## ingredients

2 tablespoons vegetable oil
2 onions, chopped
2 cloves garlic, chopped
2½ cm fresh ginger, finely chopped
1 stick cinnamon
¼ teaspoon ground cloves
3 cardamom pods
600 g lamb, cut into cubes
1 tablespoon cumin
1 tablespoon ground coriander
4 tablespoons natural yoghurt
2 tablespoons tomato paste
1 cup beef stock
salt and freshly ground black pepper
500 g spinach, finely chopped
2 tablespoons almonds, roasted and
  flaked
**serves 4**

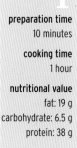

**preparation time**
10 minutes

**cooking time**
1 hour

**nutritional value**
fat: 19 g
carbohydrate: 6.5 g
protein: 38 g

1 Heat the oil in a flameproof casserole dish or large, heavy-based saucepan. Fry onions, garlic, ginger, cinnamon, cloves and cardamom for 5 minutes until onions and garlic are soft and spices are fragrant.

2 Add lamb and fry for 5 minutes, turning, until it begins to colour. Mix in cumin and coriander, then add the yoghurt 1 tablespoon at a time, stirring well each time.

3 Mix together the tomato paste and stock and add to the lamb. Season with salt and pepper. Bring to the boil, reduce heat, cover and simmer for 30 minutes or until lamb is tender.

4 Stir in spinach, cover and simmer for another 15 minutes or until mixture has reduced. Remove cinnamon stick and cardamom pods and mix in almonds.

# lamb pilau with yoghurt

## ingredients

500 g lean boneless leg lamb,
   cut into 2 cm cubes
6 cloves
8 black peppercorns
4 green cardamom pods
1 teaspoon cumin seeds
2½ cm stick cinnamon
1 tablespoon coriander seeds
2 small red chillies
5 cups water
2 tablespoons ghee or oil
1 onion, finely chopped
3 cm fresh ginger, grated
2 cloves garlic, crushed
500 g basmati rice, soaked for
   30 minutes in enough water
   to cover
½ teaspoon salt
lemon, to garnish
yoghurt, to serve
**serves 4-6**

1 Put lamb cubes in a saucepan. Tie cloves, peppercorns, cardamom pods, cumin seeds, cinnamon, coriander seeds and chillies in a muslin bag and add to pan with the water.

2 Bring to a boil, lower heat and simmer for 40 minutes or until meat is very tender. Strain, reserving lamb cubes and stock but discarding spice bag.

3 Heat ghee or oil in a large frying pan, add onion, ginger and garlic, and fry for 2 minutes, stirring frequently.

4 Add lamb cubes, stirring to coat them in spices. Cook for 10 minutes until golden brown.

5 Meanwhile, drain the rice and transfer to a large saucepan. Pour in enough reserved stock to cover rice by about 4 cm. Add salt. Bring to a boil, reduce heat, cover and cook for 10–15 minutes or until rice is almost tender and most of the stock has been absorbed.

6 Add rice to meat mixture in pan and fork through lightly. Cover tightly and cook over very low heat until rice is tender, adding more stock if necessary. Garnish with lemon and serve with yoghurt.

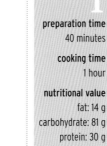

**i**

**preparation time**
40 minutes

**cooking time**
1 hour

**nutritional value**
fat: 14 g
carbohydrate: 81 g
protein: 30 g

# madras curry

## ingredients

30 g plain flour
salt and freshly ground black pepper
500 g stewing steak, cut into 2 cm
   cubes
55 g ghee or 4 tablespoons oil
2 onions, finely chopped
1 teaspoon turmeric
1 teaspoon ground coriander
1 teaspoon cayenne pepper
½ teaspoon ground black mustard
   seeds
½ teaspoon cumin
2 cloves garlic, crushed
145 ml hot water
55 g seedless raisins
**serves 4**

1 Place the flour in a plastic bag and season with salt and pepper. Add stewing steak, close bag and shake until evenly coated.

**preparation time**
6 minutes

**cooking time**
2 hours 35 minutes

**nutritional value**
fat: 20 g
carbohydrate: 18 g
protein: 28 g

2 Heat ghee or oil in a heavy-based pan, add floured beef cubes and fry for 5 minutes, stirring and turning meat so that all sides are browned.

3 Add onions and cook, stirring occasionally, for 5 minutes longer.

4 Stir in spices and cook for 3 minutes, then add garlic. Cook for 2 minutes.

5 Add the hot water. Bring to a boil and boil briskly, stirring constantly, for 5 minutes.

6 Stir in the raisins and add more water, if necessary, to cover meat. Bring to the boil, reduce heat and simmer for 2¼ hours, adding more water as required. Serve at once or cool swiftly, refrigerate and reheat next day.

# meatballs in tomato sauce

### ingredients

500 g minced lamb
5 tablespoons natural yoghurt
5 cm fresh ginger, finely chopped
1 green chilli, deseeded and finely
   chopped
3 tablespoons coriander leaves,
   chopped
2 teaspoons cumin
2 teaspoons ground coriander
salt and black pepper
2 tablespoons vegetable oil
1 onion, chopped
2 cloves garlic, chopped
½ teaspoon turmeric
1 teaspoon garam masala
1 tablespoon water
400 g can chopped tomatoes
**serves 4**

*i*

**preparation time**
20 minutes

**cooking time**
50 minutes

**nutritional value**
fat: 22.5 g
carbohydrate: 6 g
protein: 28 g

1 Mix the lamb, 1 tablespoon of yoghurt, ginger, chilli, 2 tablespoons of coriander, cumin and ground coriander and salt and pepper. Shape the mixture into 16 meatballs.

2 Heat 1 tablespoon of oil in a large saucepan, then fry meatballs for 10 minutes, turning until browned. You may have to cook them in batches. Drain on kitchen towel and set aside.

3 Heat the remaining oil in the pan. Add onion and garlic and fry for 5 minutes or until softened, stirring occasionally. Mix turmeric and garam masala with water, then add to onion and garlic. Add remaining yoghurt, 1 tablespoon at a time.

4 Add tomatoes, meatballs and 150 ml of water to mixture, and bring to a boil. Partly cover the pan, reduce heat and simmer for 30 minutes, stirring occasionally. Sprinkle rest of the coriander leaves over to garnish.

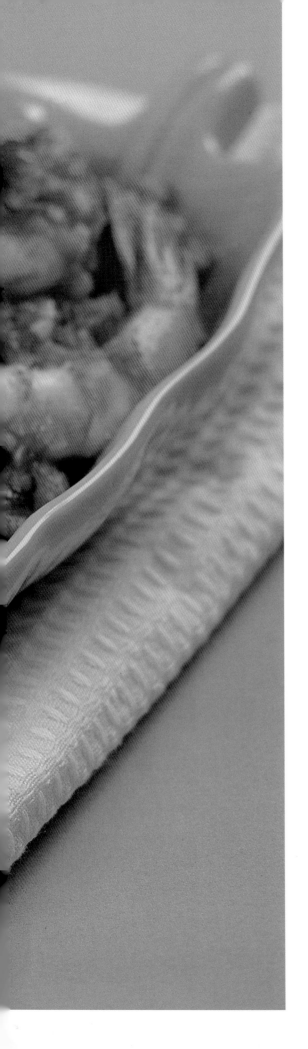

# seafood

# tikka skewers

## ingredients

550 g firm white fish fillets,
  cut into 2 cm wide strips
1 lemon, cut into wedges
*spicy yoghurt marinade*
1 small onion, chopped
3 cloves garlic, crushed
2 teaspoons fresh ginger, finely grated
1 tablespoon cumin
1 tablespoon garam masala
2 cardamom pods, crushed
1 teaspoon turmeric
1 teaspoon chilli powder
2 teaspoons ground coriander
½ tablespoon tomato paste
1¼ cups natural yoghurt
*cucumber raita*
1 cucumber, finely chopped
1 tablespoon mint leaves, chopped
1 cup natural yoghurt
**serves 4**

**i**

**preparation time**
3 hours
refrigeration
30 minutes

**cooking time**
6 minutes

**nutritional value**
fat: 7 g
carbohydrate: 8 g
protein: 32 g

1 Pierce fish strips several times with a fork and place in a shallow glass or ceramic dish.

2 To make the marinade, place onion, garlic, ginger, cumin, garam masala, cardamom, turmeric, chilli powder, coriander and tomato paste in a food processor or blender and process until smooth. Add yoghurt and mix to combine. Spoon marinade over fish, toss to combine, cover and marinate in refrigerator for 3 hours.

3 Preheat a barbecue to medium heat. Drain fish and thread onto lightly oiled skewers. Place skewers on lightly oiled barbecue and cook, turning several times, for 5–6 minutes or until fish is cooked.

4 To make raita, place cucumber, mint and yoghurt in a bowl and mix to combine. Serve skewers with lemon wedges and raita.

vegetable dishes. Ground coriander has a distinctive taste. Don't get carried away and add too much to food or it will be overpowering.

**cube:** to cut into small pieces with six even sides; e.g. cubes of meat.

**cumin (jeera):** This spice is used both as whole seeds and ground. The whole black seeds have a sweet herbal taste and are used in northern and Moglai dishes and in biriyanis. The white or green seeds are used whole or ground cumin has a gentle flavour and is used in appetisers, snacks, batters and yoghurts.

**cut in:** to combine fat and flour using two knives scissor fashion or with a pastry blender, to make pastry.

**fennel (saunf):** fennel seeds are similar to white cumin seeds and are used mainly in pickles, drinks and rice dishes. Fennel seeds are also used to aid digestion after eating. Ground fennel is used in meat, chicken and fish dishes and gives a tangy, almost minty bite.

**fenugreek (methi):** the seeds, mainly used in lentil and some vegetable dishes, have a bitter taste. Ground fenugreek is used mainly in meat, chicken and fish dishes. Fenugreek leaves can be bought fresh or dried and are used as a flavouring for vegetables or as a herb. They have a bittersweet taste.

**fillet:** a piece of prime meat, fish or poultry which is boneless or has all bones removed.

**flake:** to separate cooked fish into flakes, removing any bones and skin, using forks.

**flame:** to ignite warmed alcohol over food or to pour into a pan with food, ignite, then serve.

**garam masala:** the name means 'mixed spice' and it consists of cinnamon, cloves, cardamom, cumin, nutmeg, black peppercorns and coriander ground together. It can be bought ready-mixed in the spice section of most supermarkets or you can make your own (page 6).

**garlic (lahsun):** this is the root of a plant and is a very important ingredient in non-vegetarian dishes, some lentil dishes and chutneys.

**ginger (adrak):** used both fresh and ground, ginger is the aromatic root of a tropical plant. Fresh ginger is a must in all Indian cooking. It has to be peeled before use. Ground ginger is used mainly as a topping with other dry spices for salads, fried vegetables and sweet dishes.

**grease:** to rub the surface of a metal or heatproof dish with oil or fat, to prevent the food from sticking.

**infuse:** to steep foods in a liquid until the liquid absorbs their flavour.

**joint:** to cut poultry and game into serving pieces by dividing at the joint.

**knead:** to work a yeast dough in a pressing, stretching and folding motion with the heel of the hand until smooth and elastic, to develop the gluten strands. Non-yeast doughs should be lightly and quickly handled as gluten development is not desired.

**line:** to cover the inside of a baking tin with paper for the easy removal of the cooked product from the baking tin.

**mango powder (amchur):** this is a brownish powder made from sun-dried green mangoes. It has a sour taste and imparts a unique flavour which is loved all over India.

**marinade:** a flavoured liquid, into which food is placed for some time to give it flavour and to tenderise. Marinades generally include an acid ingredient such as vinegar or wine, oil and seasonings.

**mustard seeds (rai):** these come in three colours: black, brown and yellow. Black mustard seeds are used mainly in vegetarian sauces, to flavour yoghurt and in vegetable dishes. Brown mustard seeds are more difficult to find but are used in chutneys and toppings. Yellow mustard seeds are used in lentil and vegetable dishes with a tomato base.

**nutmeg (jaiphal):** this spice is used in small quantities to give a subtle flavour to meat and rice dishes. It is also used in sweets and puddings.

**pan-fry:** to fry foods in a small amount of fat or oil, sufficient to coat the base of the pan.

**paprika:** this spice is used mainly as a topping for salads.

**parboil:** to boil until partially cooked. The food is then finished by some other method.

**poppy seeds (khus-khus):** these are used as a thickening agent in desserts and give a special texture to food.

**pound:** to flatten meats with a meat mallet; to reduce to a paste or small particles with a mortar and pestle.

**saffron (kesar):** this is a very expensive spice which comes from Kashmir or Spain. It has an aromatic flavour and is used to colour desserts and rice dishes.

**sesame seeds (til):** these are mainly used in chutneys, pickles and in some sweets.

**simmer:** to cook in liquid just below boiling point at about 96°C (205°F), with small bubbles rising gently to the surface.

**skim:** to remove fat or froth from the surface of simmering food.

**stock:** the liquid produced when meat, poultry, fish or vegetables have been simmered in water to extract the flavour. Used as a base for soups, sauces, casseroles, and so on. Ready-made stock is available.

**sweat:** to cook sliced onions or vegetables in a small amount of butter in a covered pan over low heat, to soften them and release flavour without colouring.

**turmeric (haldi):** an aromatic, pungent root. It is used ground to colour and flavour meat and vegetable dishes. Take care when using turmeric, as it can stain.

# conversions

easurements differ from country to country, it's important to understand what the differences are. This gives you simple 'at-a-glance' information for using the recipes in this book, wherever you may be. Cooking is not an exact science – minor variations in measurements won't make a difference to your cooking.

## equipment
The size of measuring spoons and cups used internationally differs slightly by about 2–3 teaspoons. We use the Australian standard metric measurements in our recipes:

**1 teaspoon = 5 ml**  **1 tablespoon = 20 ml**

**1/2 cup = 125 ml**  **1 cup = 250 ml**

**4 cups = 1 litre**

Measuring cups come in sets of one cup (250 ml), 1/2 cup (125 ml), 1/3 cup (80 ml) and 1/4 cup (60 ml). Use these for measuring liquids and certain dry ingredients.

Measuring spoons come in a set of four and should be used for measuring dry and liquid ingredients and guide.

When using cup or spoon measures always make them level unless the recipe indicates otherwise.

## dry versus wet ingredients
While this system of measures is consistent for liquids, it's more difficult to quantify dry ingredients. For instance, one level cup equals: 200 g of brown sugar; 210 g of caster sugar; and 110 g of icing sugar.

When measuring dry ingredients such as flour, don't push the flour down or shake it into the cup. It is best just to spoon the flour in until it reaches the desired amount. When measuring liquids, use a clear vessel indicating metric levels.

Always use medium eggs (55–60 g) when eggs are required in a recipe.

## dry

| metric (grams) | imperial (ounces) |
|---|---|
| 30 g | 1 oz |
| 60 g | 2 oz |
| 90 g | 3 oz |
| 100 g | 3 1/2 oz |
| 125 g | 4 oz |
| 150 g | 5 oz |
| 185 g | 6 oz |
| 200 g | 7 oz |
| 250 g | 8 oz |
| 280 g | 9 oz |
| 315 g | 10 oz |
| 330 g | 11 oz |
| 370 g | 12 oz |
| 400 g | 13 oz |
| 440 g | 14 oz |
| 470 g | 15 oz |
| 500 g | 16 oz (1 lb) |
| 750 g | 24 oz (1 1/2 lb) |
| 1000 g (1 kg) | 32 oz (2 lb) |

## liquids

| metric (millilitres) | imperial (fluid ounces) |
|---|---|
| 30 ml | 1 fl oz |
| 60 ml | 2 fl oz |
| 90 ml | 3 fl oz |
| 100 ml | 3 1/2 fl oz |
| 125 ml | 4 fl oz |
| 150 ml | 5 fl oz |
| 190 ml | 6 fl oz |
| 250 ml | 8 fl oz |
| 300 ml | 10 fl oz |
| 500 ml | 16 fl oz |
| 600 ml | 20 fl oz  (1 pint)* |
| 1000 ml (1 litre) | 32 fl oz |

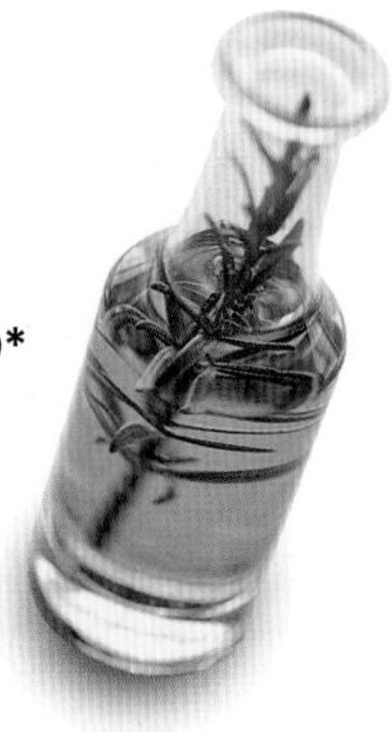

*Note: an American pint is 16 fl oz.

### oven
Your oven should always be at the right temperature before placing the food in it to be cooked. Note that if your oven doesn't have a fan you may need to cook food for a little longer.

### microwave
It is difficult to give an exact cooking time for microwave cooking. It is best to watch what you are cooking closely to monitor its progress.

### standing time
Many foods continue to cook when you take them out of the oven or microwave. If a recipe states that the food needs to 'stand' after cooking, be sure not to overcook the dish.

### can sizes
The can sizes available in your supermarket or grocery store may not be the same as specified in the recipe. Don't worry if there is a small variation in size – it's unlikely to make a difference to the end result.

| cooking temperatures | °C (celsius) | °F (fahrenheit) | gas mark |
|---|---|---|---|
| very slow | 120 | 250 | 1/2 |
| slow | 150 | 300 | 2 |
| moderately slow | 160 | 315 | 2-3 |
| moderate | 180 | 350 | 4 |
| moderate hot | 190 | 375 | 5 |
|  | 200 | 400 | 6 |
| hot | 220 | 425 | 7 |
| very hot | 230 | 450 | 8 |
|  | 240 | 475 | 9 |
|  | 250 | 500 | 10 |

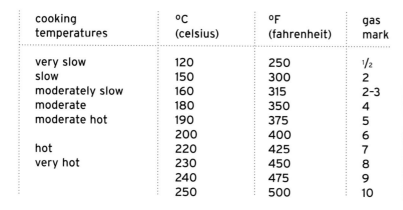

# index